# BECKETT AND DIALECTICS

ALSO AVAILABLE FROM BLOOMSBURY

*Beckett, Lacan and the Mathematical Writing of the Real*, Arka Chattopadhyay
*Revisioning Beckett: Samuel Beckett's Decadent Turn*, S. E. Gontarski
*Beckett's Words: The Promise of Happiness in a Time of Mourning*,
David Kleinberg-Levin

# BECKETT AND DIALECTICS

*Be it Something or Nothing*

### EDITED BY EVA HEUBACH

BLOOMSBURY ACADEMIC
LONDON • NEW YORK • OXFORD • NEW DELHI • SYDNEY

BLOOMSBURY ACADEMIC
Bloomsbury Publishing Plc
50 Bedford Square, London, WC1B 3DP, UK
1385 Broadway, New York, NY 10018, USA
29 Earlsfort Terrace, Dublin 2, Ireland

BLOOMSBURY, BLOOMSBURY ACADEMIC and the Diana logo
are trademarks of Bloomsbury Publishing Plc

First published in Great Britain 2021
This paperback edition published in 2022

Copyright © Eva Heubach and Contributors, 2021

Eva Heubach has asserted her right under the Copyright, Designs
and Patents Act, 1988, to be identified as Editor of this work.

For legal purposes the Acknowledgments on p. vi constitute
an extension of this copyright page.

Cover design by Charlotte Daniels
Cover image: Samuel Beckett (1986)
(© Ullstein Bild / Getty Images)

All rights reserved. No part of this publication may be reproduced or
transmitted in any form or by any means, electronic or mechanical, including
photocopying, recording, or any information storage or retrieval system,
without prior permission in writing from the publishers.

Bloomsbury Publishing Plc does not have any control over, or responsibility for, any
third-party websites referred to or in this book. All internet addresses given in
this book were correct at the time of going to press. The author and publisher
regret any inconvenience caused if addresses have changed or sites have
ceased to exist, but can accept no responsibility for any such changes.

A catalogue record for this book is available from the British Library.

A catalog record for this book is available from the Library of Congress.

| ISBN: | HB: | 978-1-3501-3683-0 |
| --- | --- | --- |
| | PB: | 978-1-3502-1436-1 |
| | ePDF: | 978-1-3501-3684-7 |
| | eBook: | 978-1-3501-3685-4 |

Typeset by Integra Software Private Limited

To find out more about our authors and books visit www.bloomsbury.com
and sign up for our newsletters.

# CONTENTS

*Acknowledgments* vi

I     Introduction 1
       Eva Heubach

II    Samuel Beckett's Method 11
       Alain Badiou

III   Two Shades of Gray 27
       Mladen Dolar

IV   Senile Dialectic 61
       Rebecca Comay

V     Beckett's *Unnamable* Realism 105
       Eva Heubach

VI   *Watt* Forms Life: Beckett and the Theory of the Novel 143
       Philipp Weber

VII   No Louder: Beckett and the Dynamics of Monotony 173
       Tadej Troha

*Notes on Contributors* 194

*Index* 196

# ACKNOWLEDGMENTS

The editor would like to thank Lucy Russell and Lisa Goodrum for their consistent enthusiasm and patience throughout the preparation of this volume, and Liza Thompson for first commissioning it. The editor would also like to acknowledge the support of the Friedrich Schlegel Graduate School of Literary Studies of Freie Universität Berlin and the German Department of Yale University for the financing of two events that eventually led up to the composition of this volume.

# I

# Introduction

## Eva Heubach

The title of this volume—*Beckett and Dialectics*—brings into connection two terms, namely, "Beckett" and "Dialectics," by linking them through the means of an ordinary "and." In doing so, it immediately elicits a very legitimate question: Of what nature should this supposed connection between Beckett and Dialectics be?

Two possible answers come to mind, the first of which would go as follows: The first term of the posited equation ("Beckett") already implies the second one ("Dialectics"). In this understanding, Dialectics would be something like a theme or a structure to be looked for and found within Beckett's texts. Hence the second term would only make explicit what was always already implied in the first one. Next to this logic of implication, another possible answer could adhere to a logic of addition, suggesting that the second term ("Dialectics") was merely added to the first one ("Beckett"). With Dialectics, one would thus apply something external to Beckett, as neither Beckett's individual texts nor his entire project would be of dialectical nature in themselves, but could be read by 'using' Dialectics as a possible 'method' of reading.

While it may seem obvious that these two possible answers represent two strictly opposing propositions as to the alleged connection between Beckett and Dialectics, it is nonetheless true that both of them are based on one fundamental common assumption. This assumption is, quite simply, that *there is* a relation. As antithetical as these two answers might be, they still both take it as given that, indeed, there is a relation between "Beckett" and "Dialectics"—the only difference being that the first answer takes this relation to be an internal one, whereas the second answer conceptualizes it as external. The premise of this volume is, however, that there is a third option.

A small anecdote that may serve as an entry point into the exploration of precisely this purported third option can be found in Adorno's essay "Titles." Here Adorno writes that his publisher, Peter Suhrkamp, always had a particular distaste for precisely the kind of title we are dealing with. The reason for "Suhrkamp's idiosyncrasies […] directed against titles with the word 'and'" was his belief that "as in allegorical interpretation, the 'and' permits everything to be connected with everything else and is thus incapable of hitting the mark."[1] According to this opinion, titles like the one we are dealing with are thus always under the suspicion of naively and even arbitrarily connecting terms that, as of themselves, might very well have no connection whatsoever. They might suggest a link, where there is no link at all, and consequently might create a topic that isn't even a topic. Ultimately, the charge brought against such "titles with the word 'and,'" is that they allow for a fabrication of something, where, simply put, there is nothing there. Does this charge also hold for the title of this very volume? Is the title "Beckett and Dialectics" guilty of relating two terms that are utterly alien to each other? Should this be the asserted third option? If the relation between "Beckett" and "Dialectics" is neither internal nor external, should the third option be that, simply put, there is no relation whatsoever?

As paradoxical as this may seem: Yes, the premise of this volume is precisely that there is no relation between "Beckett" and "Dialectics"—the whole question being, how to understand this very concept of *a relation that is not (there)*. To be able to answer this question, the contributions of the present volume shift the focus: In the phrase "there is no relation between Beckett and Dialectics," they emphasize the "there is" and thus show that what we are dealing with is *not* a simple relation between two terms, *nor* is it simply not a relation between two terms. Rather we are confronted with *a paradoxical third option* resulting from this very dilemma – namely that of *an active non-relation*.[2] The German language offers a helpful prefix precisely for this peculiar kind of relation which relies on a determinate negation—a prefix that, as we will see, Beckett himself made formidable use of: It is an *Un*-relation.

———

To make this logic graspable, we should turn to the second part of this volume's title: *Be it something or nothing*. In his famous German letter from 1937 to German publisher Axel Kaun, Beckett uses this formula to frame the peculiar "object" that contemporary literature, including his own, must aim for:

> And more and more my language appears to me like a veil which one has to tear apart in order to get to those things (or the

nothingness) lying behind it. [...] It is to be hoped the time will come, thank God, in some circles it already has, when language is best used where it is most efficiently abused. Since we cannot dismiss it all at once, at least we do not want to leave anything undone that may contribute to its disrepute. To drill one hole after another into it until that which lurks behind, be it something or nothing, starts seeping through—I cannot imagine a higher goal for today's writer.[3]

The first thing to gather from this famous quote is that language for Beckett is not simply a transparent means of communication, but rather a "veil." On the one hand, this veil covers up "that which lurks behind" ("das Dahinterkauernde," as the German original has it); it obscures and blocks the immediate access to this "object." On the other hand, this veil that is language is precisely that which generates this "object" in the first place because, of whatever nature this "behind" of language may be, it can, of course, only come into existence insofar as language as its "veil" obscures it.[4] This implies a peculiar temporal twist: a "before" language that only comes into existence retroactively, after (always already) being veiled. The "object" of modern literature is thus situated at a veritable material and logical (*top*ological as much as *chron*ological) deadlock. It is not "something" internal to language (since it is being veiled by it), but not "something" external to it either (since it is only brought into existence through the very act of its veiling); it is "something" inside of language that is "something" else than language – all the while only coming into existence through language itself.

What one can thus derive from Beckett's German letter is a paradoxical definition of the "highest goal" of modern literature that requires it to operate in a strangely wound structure: literature is to aim at that which is veiled by language, and it is to do so by means of language, that is, by means of this veil itself. To achieve this "highest goal," the writer is to use his working material against itself, such that he manages "to tear it apart," "to drill one hole after another into it" until the "object" that lies behind it or underlies it begins to seep through.[5] However, this formula also entails a qualification of said "object": it is no thing with positive qualities, but not nothing either; an "unnamable" thing (to use Beckett's words): "be it something or nothing."[6]

Hence there appears to be a redoubled dialectic at work in what Beckett defines as the undertaking that is literature: a dialectic between language and its peculiar object, and another one that concerns (and maybe even takes place within) this object itself; a dialectic that in its structure follows precisely the logic of *Un*-relation illustrated above.

The premise of the present volume is that Beckett in his project of a "literature of the unword"[7] conceptualizes and formalizes in a very precise, almost mathematical way the very logic of this Un-relation within language—within "the unnature of the word"[8]—and within the peculiar "object" pertaining to it. And furthermore, it is the premise of the present volume that it is precisely this peculiar "object" which "makes dialectics tick" in the first place.

———

It is against this background that the volume brings together the abovementioned two terms—"Beckett" and "Dialectics"—two terms that for a long time have been regarded as contradicting one another or even as being mutually exclusive. Beckett has repeatedly been read as a sort of "anti-Dialectician," an "anti-Hegel," displaying a negative teleology, in the sense that the movement of his literature "worstward ho" could be pitted against a supposed Hegelian teleology or theodicy of the "bestward ho." The aim of the present volume is, however, to sidestep this very opposition. In doing so, its intention is neither to merely regress to positions that have long been overcome nor simply to revisit previous dialectical readings of Beckett—if critical or affirmative—and to investigate them as to their continuing actuality. Rather, the aim of the present volume and the project it endorses is to resuscitate something (or nothing) from within the dialectical heritage that might offer the means for a reconfiguration and maybe a renewal of what dialectical thinking is to mean—and to do this precisely by *working with* and *working through* Beckett.

This endeavor by no means entails a disregard or neglect of the important structuralist or poststructuralist readings of Beckett. The framework of the present volume rather starts from the assumption that Beckett should be considered and taken to be an autonomous position within structuralism and the structuralist discussion itself—a position which can demonstrate in what way structuralism indeed *is* dialectic.

How is this to be understood? If structuralism has taught us one thing, it is first and foremost that language operates as a system of pure differentiality. In language, there are only differences without positive terms, since the identity of a signifier is grounded in nothing but a series of differences. Meaning only emerges through the differential relations a signifier sustains to other signifiers.[9] The crucial consequence of this differential constitution of language is that a signifier has no given positive content: it "is" nothing but the succession of what it is *not*. Yet, the further conclusion to be drawn from this insight is that the very absence of a trait can itself be taken in its positivity, in the sense that it is precisely what defines the signifier in question. In other words, if presence (the meaning of a signifier) emerges only against the backdrop of absence (as everything the signifier does not mean), the consequence is not only that absence should be taken to be primary, but also that we need to think the presence of absence as such—"be it something or nothing." In this precise sense, structuralism has made it graspable that differentiality is not only a but *the* core feature of dialectics proper.[10]

The contributions of the present volume share the intuition that Beckett's œuvre, in its very investigation of shapes, types, and forms of negation, presents an exploration of precisely this peculiar sort of (presence of) absence. Each of the contributions thus adopts a perspective that, in its singular way, pays particular attention to the structure of Beckett's texts, to its formal composition and constitution. The volume thereby openly and directly circumvents the so often prevailing tendency to either make literature prove a philosophical point or apply a theory or philosophical method upon a literary text. Instead, it takes the specific potential of literature seriously. In doing so, the following contributions not only shed new light on Beckett's work—and with it on the modernist artistic project as such. Moreover, they provide possible resources for a new understanding of the dialectical enterprise and its basic coordinates – an endeavor in which Beckett might well be our most crucial partner in crime.

# Notes

1. Theodor W. Adorno, "Titles. Paraphrases on Lessing," in *Notes to Literature*, vol. II, ed. Rolf Tiedemann, trans. Shierry Weber Nicholsen (New York: Columbia University Press, 1991), 5.

2. This is, of course, the very logic of what Lacan famously conceptualizes as the condition of the sexual relation: "There is no sexual relation." Jacques Lacan, *The Seminar, Book XVII, the Other Side of Psychoanalysis, 1969–1970*, ed. Jacques-Alain Miller, trans. Russell Grigg (London/New York: W. W. Norton & Co., 2007).

3. Samuel Beckett in a letter to Axel Kaun on July 9, 1937, in *The Letters of Samuel Beckett, Volume I: 1929–1940*, ed. Martha Dow Fehsenfeld and Lois More Overbeck (Cambridge: Cambridge University Press, 2009), 518. The German original reads as follows: "Und immer mehr wie ein Schleier kommt mit meine Sprache vor, den man zerreissen muss, um an die hinterliegenden Dinge (oder das hinterliegende Nichts) zu kommen. […] Hoffentlich kommt die Zeit, sie ist ja Gott sei Dank in gewissen Kreisen schon da, wo die Sprache da am besten gebraucht wird, wo sie am tüchtigsten missgebraucht wird. Da wir sie so mit einem Male nicht ausschalten können, wollen wir wenigstens nichts versäumen, was zu deren Verruf beitragen mag. Ein Loch nach dem andern in ihr zu bohren, bis das Dahinterkauernde, sei es etwas oder nichts, durchzusickern anfängt—ich kann mir für den heutigen Schriftsteller kein höheres Ziel vorstellen." Ibid., 513–14.

4. Ibid.

5. Ibid.

6   Ibid.

7   Ibid., 515. This is my translation faithful to the original German "Literatur des Unworts." The English translation by Viola Westbrook in *The Letters of Samuel Beckett* reads "literature of the non-word." Ibid., 520.

8   Ibid., 518.

9   As Saussure famously puts it, "*In the language itself, there are only differences.* Even more important than that is the fact that, although in general a difference presupposes positive terms between which the difference holds, in a language there are only differences, and *no positive terms.*" Ferdinand de Saussure, *Course in General Linguistics*, ed. and trans. Roy Harris (London/New York: Bloomsbury, 2013), 140–1.

10  This is a point that has repeatedly been made and made productive by Slavoj Žižek. Cf. for example Slavoj Žižek, *Less than Nothing: Hegel and the Shadow of Dialectical Materialism* (London/New York: Verso, 2012), 582–3. Žižek refers to the conclusion drawn by Fredric Jameson, who recognizes in the rise of structuralist theory in the 1960s "a reawakening or a rediscovery of the dialectic" and in Hegel's *Phenomenology of Spirit* "a profoundly structuralist work *avant la lettre.*" Fredric Jameson, *The Hegel Variations* (London/New York: Verso, 2010), 48.

# Bibliography

Adorno, Theodor W. "Titles. Paraphrases on Lessing." In *Notes to Literature*, vol. II, edited by Rolf Tiedemann, translated by Shierry Weber Nicholsen, 3–11. New York: Columbia University Press, 1991.

Beckett, Samuel. *The Letters of Samuel Beckett, Volume I: 1929–1940*, edited by Martha Dow Fehsenfeld and Lois More Overbeck. Cambridge: Cambridge University Press, 2009.

Jameson, Fredric. *The Hegel Variations*. London/New York: Verso, 2010.

Lacan, Jacques. *The Seminar. Book XVII. The Other Side of Psychoanalysis. 1969–1970*, edited by Jacques-Alain Miller, translated by Russell Grigg. London/New York: W. W. Norton & Co., 2007.

Saussure, Ferdinand de. *Course in General Linguistics*, edited and translated by Roy Harris. London/New York: Bloomsbury, 2013.

Žižek, Slavoj. *Less than Nothing. Hegel and the Shadow of Dialectical Materialism.* London/New York: Verso, 2012.

# II

# Samuel Beckett's Method

## Alain Badiou

### Translated by Eva Heubach

There is a somewhat rational development in the writings of Samuel Beckett. I think one can, broadly speaking, discern three periods.

1. During the 1940s and 1950s, Beckett publishes what can still carry the subtitle "novel." There is, in any case, a narrative, a (hi)story, and identifiable characters, endowed with some consistency. However, these characters are increasingly typified: as an example, just compare the named characters portrayed in *Watt*, or even in *Molloy*, to the buried subject of *The Unnamable*.

2. In the sixties and seventies, I would say that Beckett instead turns to *fables*: the localization of "what is going on" is abstract, and the living beings populating these places are functions rather than characters. The purely visible and the designation prevail over the story and consciousness. Let us name as an example *The Lost Ones*, or *How It Is*.

3   During the end of the seventies and the eighties, we are definitely dealing with *allegories*. Language must capture the visible and subject it to its questions, which is why the poem prevails over the prose.

On another occasion, I have spoken, with regard to Samuel Beckett's prose-work after *How It Is*, of a latent poem. As if, to undo the novel, the novelistic, in the end, there is nothing but the poem. And as if, to nonetheless defend the prose, in the end, the ultimate resource would be to conceal the poem. Therefore, the latent poem. But what does that say? What does that ill say? The latent poem, ill seen under the prose, and in it ill said. Ill seen ill said. *Ill Seen Ill Said*, a latent poem published in 1981, thirty-seven years ago, already, and nonetheless still ill understood. Ill read ill said again [*Mal lu mal redit*]. This text will serve us as a landmark to speak of a certain discourse on method that is immanent in the final works of Beckett.

In *Ill Seen Ill Said*, the prose desires to see the blackness, and thus desires to see, what cannot be seen.

> Seeing the black night or better blackness pure and simple that limpid they would shed. Blackness in its might at last. Where no more to be seen. Perforce to be seen.[1]

And prose also desires to name the unnamable. For example, the haze that the eye becomes when it does not see anymore:

> The eye will close in vain. To see but haze. Not even. Be itself but haze. How can it ever be said? Quick how ever ill said before it submerges all. Light. In one treacherous word. Dazzling haze.

Light in its might at last. Where no more to be seen. To be said. Gently gently. [*Du calme.*]²

Yes, gently [*du calme*], because the point where it is said that there is nothing to be said and seen that there is nothing to be seen, the endpoint, all in all, is the void. It is this point that puts an end to the latent poem. The last sentences of this latent poem from a third of a century ago, *Ill Seen Ill Said*:

One moment more. One last. Grace to breath that void. Know happiness.³

But it is a difficult achievement to arrive at this point, thus to know happiness. Between difficult and impossible, between the subject and happiness, there is all the thrust that the latent poem exerts on the prose. The thrust of the being-written [*l'être-écrit*] on and in the written-appearance [*l'apparaître-écrit*]. The order of the writing is the discipline of this thrust, and Beckett's invention is the deliberate creation of this discipline. In three stages. First, from *Murphy* to *Molloy* via *Watt*—the formalism of the circumstances. Then from *Molloy* to *How It Is* via *The Unnamable*—the rational terror of the subject. Then from *How It Is* to *Stirrings Still* through *The Lost Ones* and *Ill Seen Ill Said*, the latent poem has reached its explicit form, passed over from being to appearance [*de l'être à l'apparaître*]. Thus, little by little, the discipline of a prosodic and figurative asceticism. The texts are short and cut up in verses. The artificial components of the visible are reduced to testimonies. In *Ill Seen Ill Said*, there is the "old deal spindlebacked kitchen chair"⁴; the buttonhook: "Of tarnished silver pisciform it hangs by its hook from a nail"⁵; the pallet: "scarce to be seen"[6]; the antique coffer: "Far from it in a corner see suddenly an antique coffer. In its therefore no lesser solitude."[7] And a trapdoor: "Still fresh the coffer fiasco what now of all things but a trapdoor."[8] And the clock: "Close-up of a dial," with "one hand only" that "leaps from dot to dot with so lightning a leap that but for its new position it had not stirred."[9] Total discrete of things.

Let us note in passing that the space [l'espace] in Beckett's theater is always practically uniform, indistinct and that in this space, the scene [le lieu] is entirely defined by an extremely strict list of objects. On this specific point, Beckett closely monitored the performances and prohibited any proliferation of objects, just as any aspect of decoration of the space. Likewise, in his films, everything takes form in front of a uniform background, a wall, for example, or even better, the blackness of a crossfading plane. In *Ill Seen Ill Said*, the space is reduced to elementary surfaces. The stones and weeds are organized without any imputable limit around a single cabin. A disguised citation from Pascal introduces the description, since the cabin is situated "at the inexistent centre of a formless space."[10] There, "stones increasingly abound. Ever scanter even the rankest weed."[11] This space is rather circular, surrounded by the invisible sea ("Gone she hears one night the sea as if afar.").[12]

Finally, the living beings that populate the space form a kind of rigorous choral composition. This holds already for the theater; if the basic structure is not that of a monologue, as in *Happy Days* or *Krapp's Last Tape*, it can only be that of a duo, as in *Waiting for Godot* or *Endgame*. Some secondary characters are never more than intercalations that relaunch these privileged structures. In *Ill Seen Ill*

*Said*, there is the rigid woman in black, whose gaze fills the sublime opening in its entirety:

> From where she lies she sees Venus rise. On. From where she lies when the skies are clear she sees Venus rise followed by the sun. Then she rails at the source of all life. On. At evening when the skies are clear she savours its star's revenge. At the other window. Rigid upright on her old chair she watches for the radiant one.[13]

This woman who rails at the source of all life occupies the place of the objective Subject, of the hero, in the Beckettian sense: he or she who measures the withdrawing of sense [*retrait du sens*] and the hypothesis of truth [*l'assomption de la vérité*]. Under his eye, there are the others, of which the text decides that they, just as the apostles, are twelve. A literary decision, taken in response to the question of a potential eradication of man:

> And man? Shut of at last? Alas no. For will she not be surprised one day to find him gone? Surprised no she is beyond surprise. How many? A figure come what may. Twelve. Wherewith to furnish the horizon's narrow round.[14]

And in this register of the living, in addition to the subject and the others, there are finally the animals, here lambs and ewes:

> And what lambs. No trace of frolic. White splotches in the grass. Aloof from the unheeding ewes. Still. Then a moment straying. Then still again. To think there is still life in this age. Gently gently. [*Du calme*][15]

Gently [*Du calme*], because to say what a living human subject is, is a task doomed to fail in the latent poem, which is why one must proceed by simplification, the first one being, as in theater or cinema, to bring everything back to the dialectic of immobility and movement. However, underneath it all, this subject is able to see the stars, often brought back to the trilogy of the sun, the moon, and the Venus. Rigid stars that move the subject from one window of the cabin to another, as if it was the ocean that pulled, astral, the tide of destiny. The necessity of the visible that is all the more constraining as the frozen arrangement of the stars composes, at the farthest, a landscape à la Mallarmé.

> Moonless star-studded sky reflected in the erosions filmed with ice.[16]

We thus have the enumerable totality of a cosmos. For Beckett cannot, just as his master Dante, situate the thrust of the poem anywhere else than in the maniac arrangement of the strata of the world. From one book to another, from *Watt* to *Stirrings Still*, we can follow the avatars of the Beckettian cosmology. In *Ill Seen Ill Said* we can thus enumerate its nine components:

1. The stars
2. Sun, Venus, and Moon
3. The invisible sea that surrounds the earth
4. The circular earth of stones and weeds
5. Generic living beings (ewes, lambs)

6 The others, the twelve

7 The central cabin

8 The objects

9 The character, the objective Subject

All of this is the real, the visible instituted by the prose. But at the same time, this real resists the prose it establishes because the prose desires the peace of the disappearance of all real. It desires that the saying [*le dire*] be exact, and thus that it is saying of nothing because the saying of something is inevitably an ill saying [*un mal dire*]. The real resists the prose because this opposite of the real, the nothing, cannot be said. The real demands that the prose continues eternally, simply because no opposite of the real is sayable:

> Such the confusion now between real and—how say its contrary? No matter. That old tandem. […] Such equal liars both. Real and—how ill say its contrary? The counter-poison.[17]

The counter-poison of the real is the real itself, as nothing, as void. The prose under the pressure of the poem desires the void as dialecticization of the real [*la mise en dialectique du reel*], as its submission to the power of the negative, as that which doesn't have to be seen nor said anymore, since it is at the same time the real and its annulment. Sometimes Beckett dreams of the irruption of the nothing (the black, the void) as of a moment of redemption:

> But black. Void. Nothing else. […] Gently gently. [*Du calme.*][18]
> Incontinent the void. The zenith.[19]

This logic of the void that completes the cosmology in the recurrence of the annihilation of the world will be fully unfolded in *Worstward Ho*, where Beckett will distinguish between the Black and the Dim.

However, in *Ill Seen Ill Said*, the cosmos' ingredients are still of the order of contingent appearance. In reality, the cosmos is a decor; the character itself is an external object. We remain at the level of description, thus, at the level of the prose. Yet the poem is the latent declaration concealing a description; it is the true dramaturgy of the real beneath the contingent and artificial animation of the cosmos. One must move beyond all description, and those are the stakes of the prose-poem, just as the stakes for the theater are to move beyond the play, and those of the cinema are to go beyond the image. When we arrive at the poem, what matters is no longer the system of the strata of the visible, nor the saying of the spaces [*le dire des espaces*], the objects, and the living. What matters is the apparatus for capturing all this [*l'appareil de capture de tout cela*]. Not the seen, but the seeing [*le voir*]; not the said, but the saying [*le dire*]. Thus, the seeing as being of the ill seen and the saying as being of the ill said. On the one side, there is the eye that frames the scene; on the other, there is the question that constraints the sentence. Eye and question are the two veritable heroes of the late Beckett. They compose the subject's subjective, of which the women in black is just the shadow, the objective part. And the most intense of the poem is achieved when the eye and the question intertwine, when it comes to the question of the seeing, the name of the eye, or the seeing of language, as in this crucial passage:

> Suddenly the look. Nothing having stirred. Look? Too weak a word. Too wrong. Its absence? No better. Unspeakable globe.[20]

In theater, the problem is that of the link between what one sees and what is said. For Beckett, one always sees too much, and one speaks either not enough or too much. Between "too much" and "not enough," there is what Beckett calls the "question." However, the eye does not bear the question of its name. Such is the drama of the subject-subject. This drama is organized by the traversal of the cosmos according to the order of the questions and the film-like framing of the scene. To grasp its nuances, we would have to follow this order and this framing. For example, we would have to note that there are thirty questions in *Ill Seen Ill Said*. The first one:

> How come a cabin in such a place? How came? Careful. Before replying …[21]

And the last one:

> For the last time at last for to end yet again what the wrong word? Than revoked. No but slowly dispelled a little very little like the last wisps of day when the curtain closes.[22]

One initial question about the construction of the visible cosmos, one final question concerning the last saying. Either the problem of the sudden end (annulment) or the endless end (slowly dispelled a little, very little). Such is the organization of the ill saying under the constraint of the thirty questions.

The other side of this statistical access: the relation between "eye" and "seeing," tied by this phrase:

> Nothing for it but to close the eye for good and see her. Her and the rest. Close it for good and all and see her to death.[23]

One will note that the word "eye" is used fifty-five times, the verbs "see" and "see again" fifty-seven times. From the onset: "From where she lies she sees Venus rise. On."[24] Up to the last and final desire: "Blackness in its might at last. Where no more to be seen. Perforce to be seen."[25]

These purely textual considerations, and some more (yes, we, the philosophers, we care about the signifier, oh so much!), authorize us to say that the Beckettian text obeys—in *Ill Seen Ill Said* anyhow, but often elsewhere as well from *How It Is* onward—three axioms of writing.

> Axiom 1: Construct with hypothetical pieces, an elementary cosmos. Stars, fence, earth, plants, living beings, character, objects.
>
> Axiom 2: Include in the cosmos, but at a sort of inner distance, the apparatus for its capturing [*l'appareil de sa capture*]: questions in the order of the saying and eye in the order of the seeing.
>
> Axiom 3: Endeavor to join, concerning the cosmos and the little that is going on there, the ill saying of that which answers to the questions and the ill seeing of the eye's actions.

Under the jurisdiction of these axioms, there is what one can call the action of the text. On the surface, the prose, that is, the descriptive setting up of the cosmos. Of its pure present: "From where she lies she sees Venus rise."[26] Of its past: "There was a time when she did not appear in the zone of stones. A long time."[27] Just as of its future: "Empty handed she shall go to the tomb. Until she go no more. Or no more return. So much for that [*C'est décidé*]."[28]

The "So much for that [*C'est décidé*]" punctuates what is going on underneath the descriptive prose. Because underneath the description, there is what one can call the operations: the questions of the saying [*le dire*], and the framings of the eye [*cadrages de l'œil*]. These operations are the artifice of art (the poem subtracted from the pure dictatorship of the real) - this we are being taught with precision by the numerous allusions to the technical artifice, be it cinema or photography. For example, "Seated on the stones she is seen"[29] by whom, if not by the apparatus for capturing [*l'appareil de capture*] that frames her in the prose, under the thrust of the poem? And yet again, "The hands. Seen from above. They rest on the pubis intertwined."[30] That is the part of the eye. Concerning the questions, they culminate in the question about the questions.

> Was it ever over and done with questions [*où plus question de questions*]? Dead the whole brood no sooner hatched. Long before. In the egg. Long before. Over and done with answering [*plus question de répondre*]. With not being able. With not being able not to want to know. With not being able. No. Never. A dream. Question answered.[31]

As we can see, the question cannot disappear. The only hope is that we can do without an answer: "If there may not be no more questions let there at least be no more answers."[32]

Such is the purely operational stratum of the poem, underneath the repetitive stability of the cosmos. However, even underneath these operations, still, in the direction of the latent poem, there is the pure word, the injunction of the void, driving the cosmos toward its dissemination, its disappearance, *all the while retaining it in the prose*. There is the fictitious experience of the end of the world so that finally we know, in the future anterior, what it is worth. The pure word is the word that vouches for itself, and that exactly says what it says. That is why, once we have arrived at this depth, we have canticles and aphorisms.

The canticle appropriates the subject to what is becoming so that beyond cosmic appearance, one can glorify the pure being. There is thus the canticle of the end, the call for the gentle joy of the void: "Grace to breathe that void. Know happiness."[33] Or yet the call for the absolute immobility in which to melt into: "At least they appear an instant. North where she passes them always. Shroud of radiant haze. Where to melt into paradise."[34] And again: "Well on the way to inexistence. As to zero the infinite."[35] There is, as another example, the canticle of the enchanted gaze: "Rigid with face and hands against the pane she stands and marvels long."[36]

As to the aphorisms, they seek to hold on to the remnant of marvel and being, lying in the desire for the shadow and nothingness. To my mind, these are the decisive and discrete formulas in the heart of the hidden poem. They establish an irreducible point which cannot be undermined by the ascent of the shadow. In *Enough*, there is "Stony ground but not entirely."[37] The "not entirely" is the exception, which makes it possible that saying "how it is" is hell, indeed, but linked to a luminous exception, from where everything can start again. In *Ill Seen Ill Said*, from the beginning onward, from the rise of Venus, there is the illusion of life. We can oppose its disappearance in the last rays of the sun to the appearance of the second and essential clarity of the moon: "Rigid upright on her old chair she watches for the radiant one."[38] There is a smile that remains on the firm face of the women:

> Impressive above all the corners imperceptibly upcurved. A smile? Is it possible? Ghost of an ancient smile smiled finally once and for all. Such ill half seen the mouth in the light of the last rays. Suddenly they leave it. Rather it leaves them. Off again to the dark. There to smile on. If smile is what it is.[39]

These moments of radiant revenge or of the eternal smile find in *Ill Seen Ill Said* a form of an abstract aphorism, quite parallel to that of *Enough*: "Absence supreme good and yet."[40] In the heart of the latent poem, everything hangs on the "and yet." The "and yet," for its part, hangs on the tenacity of the trace, the trace of the smile, of the enchantment, of the radiant. Let us listen to the desire and the power of the exception. Let us listen to them in the murmur of the prose, which is itself through its sonority exposed to the irrepressible poetic thrust, where every exception seeks the untraceable name of its survival:

> Absence supreme good and yet. Illumination then go again and on return no more trace. On earth's face. Of what was never. [*De l'illusion.*] And if by mishap some left then go again. For good

again. So on. Till no more trace. On earth's face. Instead of always the same place. Slaving away forever in the same place. At this and that trace. And what if the eye could not? No more tear itself away from the remains of trace. Of what was never. [*De l'illusion.*] Quick say it suddenly can and farewell say say farewell. If only to the face. Of her tenacious trace. [*D'elle tenace trace.*][41]

"Of her tenacious trace." To hold on to the trace [*Tenir la trace*], such is the imperative that the latent poem locally imposes to the prose of the world. Against the illusion, hold on to the trace, as does the cinema when it makes itself trace rather than image.

The virtue that the exception demands from us is the tenacity in holding on to the traces. A virtue that the world undoes, constantly, today even more, in its insane appetite for illusory images. Yes, to cultivate the sense of the humble trace: that is what we must do next to Beckett, very close to him.

# Notes

1 Samuel Beckett, "Ill Seen Ill Said," in *Company, Ill Seen Ill Said, Worstward Ho, Stirrings Still*, ed. Dirk Van Hulle (London: Faber and Faber, 2009), 77.
2 Ibid., 71.
3 Ibid., 78.
4 Ibid., 45.
5 Ibid., 52.
6 Ibid., 54.
7 Ibid., 62.
8 Ibid., 66.

9   Ibid., 69.
10  Ibid., 45–6.
11  Ibid., 46.
12  Ibid., 51.
13  Ibid., 45.
14  Ibid., 47.
15  Ibid., 48.
16  Ibid., 67.
17  Ibid., 65–6.
18  Ibid., 60.
19  Ibid., 65.
20  Ibid., 76–7.
21  Ibid., 46.
22  Ibid., 78.
23  Ibid., 59.
24  Ibid., 45.
25  Ibid., 77.
26  Ibid., 45.
27  Ibid., 49.
28  Ibid., 68.
29  Ibid., 58.
30  Ibid., 60.
31  Ibid., 64.
32  Ibid., 68.
33  Ibid., 78.
34  Ibid., 58.
35  Ibid., 74.
36  Ibid., 46.
37  Samuel Beckett, "Enough," in *Texts for Nothing and Other Shorter Prose 1950–1976*, ed. Mark Nixon (London: Faber and Faber, 2009), 93.

38  Beckett, "Ill Seen Ill Said," 45.

39  Ibid., 71.

40  Ibid., 77.

41  Ibid.

# Bibliography

Beckett, Samuel. "Enough." In *The Complete Short Prose: 1929–1989*, edited by Stanley E. Gontarski, 186–92. New York: Grove Press, 1995.

Beckett, Samuel. "Ill Seen Ill Said." In *Company. Ill Seen Ill Said. Worstward Ho. Stirrings Still*, edited by Dirk Van Hulle, 43–78. London: Faber and Faber, 2009.

# III

# Two Shades of Gray

## Mladen Dolar

In the summer of 1945, Samuel Beckett famously had a revelation. The word is strong, but Beckett used it himself on a number of occasions. The circumstances were such that Beckett, after the war years, largely spent hiding in the village of Roussillon in the south of France, traveled back to Ireland to see his ailing mother whom he hadn't seen in six years. And there, in his mother's room, at the age of thirty-nine, he had the revelation that essentially marked his subsequent life and literary career.

One can quote his later literary testimony of this momentous event. In *Krapp's Last Tape* (1958), we see old Krapp, aged sixty-nine, listening to the recording he made thirty years ago, thus aged thirty-nine, which involves the "revelation."

> Spiritually a year of profound gloom and indigence until that memorable night in March, at the end of the jetty, in the howling wind, never to be forgotten, when suddenly I saw the whole thing. The vision at last. This I fancy is what I have chiefly to record this

evening, against the day when my work will be done and perhaps no place left in my memory, warm or cold, for the miracle that ... (*hesitates*) ... for the fire that set it alight. What I suddenly saw then was this, that the belief I had been going on all my life, namely—(*Krapp switches off impatiently, winds tape forward, switches on again*)—great granite rocks the foam flying up in the light of the lighthouse and the wind-gauge spinning like a propeller, clear to me at last that the dark I have always struggled with to keep under is in reality my most—(*Krapp curses, switches off, winds tape forward, switches on again*)—unshatterable association until my dissolution of storm and night with the light of the understanding and the fire.[1]

Of course, this is a fictional account, and although this may be one of Beckett's most autobiographical texts, it cannot be taken at face value. The account is on the one hand highly misleading, consciously so, and indeed it may be seen as a stroke of Beckett's peculiar wry humor to stage this momentous revelation against the romantic backdrop of the jetty, the tumultuous sea, the foam, the howling wind, the rocks, the lighthouse, the storm—it's all a red herring. Many readers were taken in by this dramatic picture designed to be iconic, speculating whether this took place in the Dublin harbor on the Dún Laoghaire jetty. But as Beckett wrote to Richard Ellmann many decades later, shortly before his death, "All the jetty and howling wind are imaginary. It happened to me, summer 1945, in my mother's little house, named New Place, across the road from Cooldrinagh."[2] So notwithstanding the incongruous

Caspar David Friedrich-like scenery, there, is on the other hand, an inflexible grain of the real in this account. In the first sentence of *Molloy*, which can be seen as an immediate offspring of this experience, allegedly conceived on the spot,[3] this is reduced to the most sober minimalistic statement: "I am in my mother's room."[4]

Krapp's account is tantalizingly fragmented, breaking off in mid-sentences, winding the tape, we only get some snippets of a narrative, the chronology is uncertain. The most frustrating part is that the crucial sentence trails off before coming to the point. It was "clear to me at last that the dark I have always struggled with to keep under is in reality my most …."[5] As Beckett told Knowlson, this is how the sentence should be continued: "the dark I have always struggled with to keep under is in reality my most precious ally."[6] So the dark is the ally, the closest friend, not something to be dispelled by light. Revelation is usually taken to be an affair of light, of lightening, of sudden enlightenment, the ray of light with the capacity to transform, to see light, as the saying goes, so this looks like an anti-revelation, a revelation of darkness, Beckett suddenly "seeing dark," as it were. The transformational power was sought in the wrong quarters, the threatening overwhelming darkness was fought instead of being espoused and welcomed—but can one ever welcome it? It seems that there can be no redemption in the dark, yet in this realm without hope and redemption, he now saw his way—but this is too quick. Rather, one would need to change the perspective to find something in the dark that escapes the stark alternative of light and dark, of salvation and damnation, hope and despair, absurdity and meaning, nihilism and the values that are supposed to fend it off. One wrong way to conceive this revelation would be to propose a "dialectical overturn" or economy: only if one is willing to go to the bottom of darkness one would find light; only the one who looks undauntedly at the worst, the most desperate, the most miserable and meaningless facets of human existence would thereby be able to find a way out of it and be redeemed. There is a teleology in this paradigm that Beckett never espoused (although some of his lines can be read in this way), namely that only the worst can yield the best, only the dark, at its deepest, can be transfigured into light. Slavoj Žižek recently labeled this stance "the Hölderlin paradigm,"[7] following the notorious lines "Wo aber Gefahr ist, wächst / Das Rettende auch," "But where danger is the saving powers grow as well," as one English translation has it (or in a popular pointed form: "where the danger is at the greatest, the deliverance is at the closest").[8] But this is precisely what Beckett tried to circumvent: his aim is rather to undo this alternative, to sidestep this economy of salvation, the spontaneous eschatology, the secret belief in magic by which the worst would be dialectically overturned by its own inner necessity. Or that the worst predicament is in itself already (the beginning of) a solution. This is not how one should go about if one is to deal with the topic "Beckett and Dialectics."

The revelation had its immediate literary consequences. Beckett started off as Joyce's follower; he wrote his first essay ("Dante … Bruno . Vico .. Joyce") in his defense and promotion, *Murphy* stood firmly on Joyce's territory, notwithstanding its originality and brilliance. But the revelation has shown a new path:

> I realised that Joyce had gone as far as he could in the direction of knowing more, [being] in control of one's material. He was always adding to it; you only have to look at his proofs to see that. I realised that my own way was in impoverishment, in lack of knowledge and in taking away, in subtracting rather than adding.⁹

This is what he told Knowlson two months before his death, but these words echo exactly what he said in an interview in 1956:

> The more Joyce knew the more he could. He's tending toward omniscience and omnipotence as an artist. I'm working with impotence, ignorance. There seems to be a kind of aesthetic axiom that expression is achievement—must be an achievement. My little exploration is that whole zone of being that has been set aside by artists as something unusable—as something by definition incompatible with art.¹⁰

So this is the essential upshot of the revelation: the art of subtraction (the concept whose fortune was made by Alain Badiou) vs. the art of addition; the infinitely expandable vs. the infinitely shrinkable; omniscience and omnipotence vs. ignorance and impotence; the apotheosis of the word vs. its impoverishment, the literature of the "unword" ("Literatur des Unworts," as Beckett put it in the famous German letter to Axel Kaun);¹¹ the writer who infinitely augments and expounds vs. the writer who endlessly takes away, in order to arrive at the "unnulable least"¹²—at "something" that cannot be further reduced, "be it something or nothing."¹³ Beckett saw that his own way was the literature of what literature usually leaves aside, the trivial, the negligible, the useless, the senseless, the way of poverty, exile, and loss—yet without for a moment falling into the trap of the absurd, nihilism and despair, and without the magic belief in the reversal.

The first decision that followed from the revelation was to start writing in French and thus to escape the "Anglo-Irish exuberance and automatisms,"[14] but this involved a lot more: to escape the tentacles of the mother tongue as the seemingly natural home ground of self-expression, of one's cultural heritage, the territory of the spontaneous and the homely.[15] The mother tongue is not an ally but a foe. But this only leads to this wider claim: language is not an ally but a foe. To write in a language where one is not at home is just a consequence of the fact that one is never at home in a language, so that mother tongue, and ultimately language as such, is but a refuge against what literature ought to do. To bore holes in language, as he famously put it in the letter to Axel Kaun, language as a veil to be torn, one should contribute to its disrepute if one cannot quite eliminate it. But this is not to say that one is thus aiming at somewhere beyond language where one may be grounded or "at home"—what seeps through the holes bored in language is that oscillation between "something or nothing," to the point of their indistinction, that serves as the title for this volume.

But to proceed more modestly: the first major text to be written in French is Beckett's "minor" novel *Mercier et Camier* (minor not to be taken as a value judgment, but perhaps in the vein of the tinge that Deleuze and Guattari have given to this word).[16] The novel was written over a few months, July–October 1946. Beckett couldn't find a publisher for it (Bordas having retracted), so it was only published in 1970, in dramatically different circumstances, after Beckett won the Nobel Prize in 1969 and under the pressure of general public to get something new in that momentum, even if old. So the beginning was to appear after the glorious peak of his literary career, as a post scriptum, an hors d'oeuvre after the oeuvre. Beckett, who by that time didn't think much of it, unwillingly undertook the English translation, which appeared in 1974, cutting it considerably in the process.[17]

I want to briefly consider this "early" text in order to disentangle from it one of Beckett's grand procedures which this text displays magisterially, and to contrast it to some other of his grand procedures that continue to tackle the same core problem but follow a different logic (or even a different "ontological stance," though not unrelated). For a reminder: Mercier and Camier undertake a journey, it is not quite clear where and with what intent. "Only one thing mattered: depart."[18] It is also not clear how—they have a bicycle, but they tend to forget it, and eventually find it demolished, reduced to a skeleton. They have a bag, but that they also always forget and misplace. They have an umbrella, but again constantly left behind. They depart by train, but return the next day, there is a to and fro, they keep leaving and returning—there is no way for them to depart, the departure is thwarted from the outset, and its failure keeps repeating itself. Quite aptly the original French title ran *Le Voyage de Mercier et Camier autour du Pot dans les Bosquets de Bondy*, where "le voyage autour du pot" is best rendered by the English phrase "beating around the bush," and "les bosquets de Bondy" is a forest north-east of Paris reputed since the Middle Ages for robbers and thieves. They separate, but they find each other again, only to be separated in the end. They keep running into guardians of the law, rangers, policemen—they manage to shuffle off the first one, but they beat the second one to death, without demur. They sometimes spend a night at Helen's, an alleged prostitute, and spend their time in bars. It is not clear who they are, although we learn in passing that Camier is some sort of investigator (a "private detective") who has an appointment with a customer, and that Mercier is married and has children. No way to write a summary, unless one is reduced to abstract formulas "leaving and staying at the same place," "turning and returning," "movement and stuckness," "repetition and not much difference." It looks as if this script ideally lends itself to existential wisdoms like "alienation of modern existence," "absurdity," "life is an endless journey without aim," "a godless world" etc., and curiously this kind of truisms often still abound in the zeitgeist around Beckett's name. And the wonderful thing is how Beckett himself staged these clichés in advance, as if in a series of preemptive strikes, e.g., "What are you musing on, Mercier? On the horror of existence, confusedly, said Mercier."[19] So this kind of critics unwittingly repeat Beckett's prompts, unwittingly assuming the role of his characters, without realizing to what extent they are a caricature of his preemptive staging. Hence Beckett's strategic and constant use of clichés.[20]

Beckett's revelation looks like an anti-revelation. Nothing is revealed, there is no catharsis, no epiphany of sense after the long and winding odyssey, there is no Ithaca waiting at the end of this journey, no course opens up when the journey ends. "The voyage is completed: the way begins," runs Lukács's canonic formula of the European novel,[21] but here the voyage never ends and no new path opens up. Or rather, the voyage has ended before even being started.[22] The implication that the voyage has ended already at the very beginning will present the explicit initial situation of so much of his later work (*Malone Dies, The Unnamable, Happy Days*, etc.). This is where we start, at the end of the journey, so many of Beckett's heroes have ended their journey already on the first page, and neither does any way begin. Beckett himself brought it to the magisterial formula: "The end is in the beginning and yet you go on."[23] The formula of the novel is nipped in the bud.

If revelation concerns darkness as the best ally, then this novel makes a point of finishing precisely on this note, like a demonstration: "Dark at its full"—this is the last sentence.[24] In French: "L' ombre se parfait."[25] Yet this "last judgment" is qualified by another shading:

> Alone he [Mercier] watched the sky go out, dark deepen to its full. He kept his eyes on the engulfed horizon, for he knew from experience what last throes it was capable of. And in the dark he could hear better too, he could hear the sounds the long day had kept from him, human murmurs for example, and the rain on the water.[26]

The dark is not dark, it is filled with throes, "sursauts" in French, it is not the opposite of light or its absence, but it reveals ("highlights") what the light cannot, it lets something emerge that was obfuscated by light, something that cannot be squeezed into the dramatic opposition of light and dark, something that light (and the search for light and enlightenment) doesn't allow us to see. There are differences smaller than differences, differences beneath the threshold of difference, and particularly not placeable in the seemingly most dramatic differences such as light and dark. The art of the indistinct will be henceforth one of Beckett's major guidelines, the exploration of the sub-difference that no difference can quite cover. Alain Badiou saw in this Beckett's fundamental ontological stance: "Reaching the truth of being requires that one think the in-separate, the in-disctinct. By contrast, what separates and distinguishes—what separates dark from light, for example—constitutes the place of non-being and of falsehood."[27] The momentous dividing lines—between salvation and damnation, light and dark, hope and despair, ultimately life and death ("It's vague, life and death," says Malone)[28]—are the places of deception and falsity, the non-true, and Mercier and Camier are on the way to another kind of truth.

Talking of salvation and damnation is not innocuous, and with Beckett, one is always but a small step away from Dante. Eric P. Levy has excavated a host of covert references to *The Divine Comedy*, which form an underlying current throughout the novel.[29] The most obvious one is a direct quotation: "*Lo bello stilo che m'ha fatto onore*," says Mercier, adding "is this a quote?" Beckett omitted this in the English version. ("No dreams or quotes at any price.")[30] The quote most tellingly comes from the momentous scene where Dante meets Virgil in the passage that runs: "You are my master and my author. You alone are he from whom I took the fair style that has done me honor."[31] Apart from the high irony of putting this line on the high style in the midst of most trivial conversation and quibbling, the style is precisely what Beckett wants to be rid of ("Grammar and style!," as he put it in the letter to Axel Kaun),[32] and in particular Joyce's grand style that has made the honor of his early works. The line is quoted as something that keeps buzzing in Mercier's head and burning his lips, something he cannot get rid of, as an intrusive "fixed idea" that keeps tormenting one and that it is so hard to keep at bay. Then there is the reference to hell in the Madden episode on the train: "Not alighting? said the old man. You're right, only the damned alight here."[33] Then there are references to a doubtful paradise with the doubtful Beatrice-Helen ("Time tending to drag, they manstuprated mildly, without fatigue. Before the blazing fire, in the twofold light of lamp and leaden day, they squirmed gently on the carpet, their naked bodies mingled, fingering and fondling with the languorous tact of hands arranging flowers, while the rain beat on the panes").[34] But all these are digressions in regard to the basic tonality and location of their travel, which is conspicuously the purgatory. Mercier and Camier, if we consider the Dante subtext, are in the eternal purgatory, they may stray away a bit, but they keep coming back, they are turning round and round in this place with no salvation or damnation. Purgatory has no exit, neither upward nor downward, it is the place of indistinction par excellence, the place of circular journey and repetition. But there is no innocent repetition, and in its loop almost imperceptibly something is produced, keeps being produced, something other and more intriguing than sense.

In later works, Beckett time and again evokes the "heroes" of his previous novels, who as if continue to live on as the shadows of the past that is never quite past and keep resurfacing in new incarnations and reminiscences. Thus, at the end of *Mercier and Camier*, we have a sudden reappearance of Watt, almost as deus ex machina, the "hero" of the previous novel. Then in a most telling spot in *The Unnamable*, the "narrator" is reminded of Mercier and Camier: "Two shapes then, oblong like man, entered into collision before me. They fell and I saw them no more. I naturally thought of the pseudocouple Mercier-Camier."[35] (This is described as an incident "that has only occurred once, so far. I await its recurrence without impatience."[36] The double appearing but once—yet Mercier alone will reappear twice later in the same novel.) So Mercier and Camier are qualified as a most curious sort of couple, and Beckett himself, as if off-handedly, here coined the major concept of the pseudocouple.[37] Are they a couple or not? Are they to be taken as two different persons, or as two sides or aspects of a "same" person? Is a person a redoubling of a person? Can a person be conceived without redoubling? In Beckett's universe pseudocouples swarm, and perhaps this figure of the pseudocouple is to be taken as one of the clues to his oeuvre.

Already in *Murphy* we have the couple of Neary and Wylie, and the critics have dug up in it a long list of other doublings: two coroners, two waitresses, two fortune-tellers, two alcoholics, two scholars, two Hindus, two men with tiny heads, two men with large heads, etc., as if Beckett was driven by a veritable compulsion to redouble. Then there is the series of most famous doubles, Vladimir and Estragon, Pozzo and Lucky, Watt and Knott (again redoubled by a whole range, Art and Con, Rose and Cerise, Cream and Berry, etc.), Molloy and Moran, Clov and Hamm, etc., etc.[38] How to read this? There is a spontaneous tendency to see in pseudocouples an instantiation of some grand oppositions so that each of the two would exemplify one of the opposites. Say body and mind (and this is the obvious way one can conceive the couple of Hamm and Clov). In *Mercier and Camier*, there is indeed something that points in this direction, namely, the strange appearance of Mr. Conaire, whose name clearly evokes *conarium*, the pineal gland on which Descartes pinned the connection between *res extensa* and *res cogitans*, the body and the mind. Mr. Conaire is most tellingly the bearer of the missed encounter:

> Before leaving me yesterday … you appointed to meet me here, at this very place, that very afternoon. I arrive, … with my invariable punctuality. I wait. Doubts gradually assail me. Can I have mistaken the place? The day? The hour? … You entice me to this place and take measures to prevent my seeing you. … You are gone. Why was I not told? No one knew. What time did you leave? No one knows. Are you expected back? No one knows.[39]

This is like a monologue of the unhappy pineal gland, unable to fulfill its mission, no match of body and mind. (And on top of it, it is the pineal gland who is the subject of doubt here.) To say nothing of the obscene associations that Monsieur Conaire carries in French.

There is furthermore conspicuously the tendency to sort out the couple into the master–slave relationship, most obviously with Pozzo and Lucky and the elusive couples in *Comment c'est* (where the whole issue is that a couple can only be set up through domination) and in *Le Dépeupleur* (*The Lost Ones*). There is the sexual doubling obvious with Willie and Winnie, but Beckett himself suggested it when at some point he compared Hamm and Clov as well as Didi and Gogo with his own relation to Suzanne Dechevaux-Dumesnil, his lifelong partner, their impossibility to either separate or stay together. The dialogues of the two tramps in *Godot* were supposedly recapturing their own dialogues on their long escape through France during the war, when they were sleeping in the barns and eating whatever they could find on the way to Roussillon. (Even Badiou mentions this in passing: "There was the long marriage with Suzanne, which, without engaging in vulgar 'biographism,' we can clearly see as a central reference for all the couples who traverse Beckett's work.")[40]

Even more at hand, there is the general inclination to see in them two parts of the same personality. One quote can suffice to sum up this tendency:

> Vladimir and Estragon have been seen as so complimentary that they might be the two halves of a single personality, the conscious and the subconscious mind. Each of these three pairs—Pozzo-Lucky; Vladimir-Estragon; Hamm-Clov—is linked by a relationship of mutual interdependence, wanting to leave each other, at war with each other, and yet dependent on each other. "*Nec tecum, nec sine te.*"[41] This is a frequent situation among people—married couples, for example—but it is also an image of the interrelatedness of the elements within a single personality, particularly if the personality is in conflict with itself.[42]

Pseudocouples abound in Beckett's work, but the very concept was suggested, invented by Beckett precisely in regard to the couple Mercier–Camier which constitutes like their paradigm. The temptation is always at hand to read into them some major opposition and thus to endow them with sense: body–mind, matter–spirit, master–slave, masculine–feminine, etc., or else to see them as an autonomization of psychic aspects of one personality (conscious–unconscious, intellect–passion, etc.). Inevitably they get invested with a multiplicity of meanings; they come to stand for a number of oppositions, even if fluidly so. But this is a temptation to be resisted, even if one cannot quite not succumb to it. There is something more elementary at stake, beyond meaning and psychology. There is something to be said for the formula "more than one, less than two." More than one, since this is not merely an extrapolation of the different hangs and conflicting components of a single person, this is not a staging of some psychic theater, no personification of the aspects of a personality; but less than two, since the two entities are not autonomous, independent and separate. The drama of the pseudocouple is no doubt that it cannot separate into two, nor can it be fused into a union, say into a relation of friendship or love. There is no friendship and love in Beckett, unless … Unless what? I have to leave the sentence suspended in the air. They cannot do the one without the other, but neither the one with the other, they are bound by a constant conflictual non-relation but which turns out to be the recalcitrant and incontrovertible kernel of their impossible relation. One divides into two, but not quite, one divides into pseudo-two, and the pseudo-two, though inseparable, cannot merge into one. (Or should one say: pseudo-one divides into pseudo-two? How can we conceive of "one" and "two" at all?)

At the end of *Watt*, in the Addenda, Arthur, the servant, laughs so much that he has to lean for support "against a passing shrub, or bush, which joined heartily in the joke."[43] He asks an old man the name of this plant and is told: "That's what we call a hardy laurel."[44] This was one of Beckett's favorite puns, evoking the two comedians Oliver Hardy and Stan Laurel, and the pun provides a certain clue.[45] Beckett loved early film comedies (to the point of having Buster Keaton in his *Film*), and he seems to have cast the Hardy–Laurel couple into some of his pseudocouples, or that he had this couple particularly in mind. Neary and Wylie, in *Murphy*, are fashioned as an enactment of the two, "thick and thin," so are Mercier ("a long hank,"[46] Laurel) and Camier (a "little fat one,"[47] Hardy). Vladimir and Estragon are "spontaneously" often played as a coupling of a thin and a fat man, although there is no indication of this in the script. But beyond this immediate allusion, one can surmise the reference to the long comedic tradition which from the outset used the mechanism of a double as one of its major levers. This stretches back to antiquity—think of Plautus's play *Maenechmi*, the comedy of twins, which Shakespeare took as the model for his *Comedy of Errors*, or of *Amphitruo*, the model followed by Molière and Kleist, among the host of others. The comedy thrives on doubles, on the replication and/or the split of the one—can the double from the very outset be best captured by the Beckettian concept of the pseudocouple? Is the double "always already" a pseudocouple? "In itself"? The best formula of it was given by Pascal: "Two faces which resemble each other, make us laugh, when together, by their resemblance, though neither of them by itself makes us laugh."[48] The beauty and the austere elegance of this line is that it tries to pin the comical by the very minimal, just by the mechanism of doubling. It brings it to this core: *one is not funny, two is funny,* but provided that two is the replication of one, its imitation, its likeness, its mimetic double, its similar twin. What happens between one and two to produce the comical effect? Not between one and two, but between two ones that don't quite add up to two, they are just clones of each other, same and different at the same time. Same difference, as the American saying goes. Where there should be difference, there is replication, a crack in the midst of the same. Two different faces are not funny, two similar ones are. So ultimately, this is neither a two nor two ones, but a split one, or shall one say the split preceding the one and the two, where both parts can neither be counted for two nor made one. The comical object emerges in their split as something irreducible to either. And what is astounding with Beckett is the way this comical object keeps tenaciously springing up, in the midst of the most miserable and trivial situations, by the mere virtue of the pseudocouple. Mercier and Camier are the doubles based on a missed encounter—the novel emblematically begins with their missed encounter, the impossibility to meet at the appointed time and place, and continues in their inflexible discrepancy, the mismatched yin and yang held together by nothing but their split.

There is something far-reaching in this minimal dispositive, which was, to be sure, already enacted in a number of ways in the long comedic tradition, but which Beckett brought to the core and to the gist, giving it a form for the twentieth century (preceded in this only by Flaubert's *Bouvard et Pécuchet* in the nineteenth). There is the minimal thesis, put in a naïve sort of way, that man is more than one and less than two—irreducible to a selfhood, inherently in "relation" to the other, not merely a fellow human, but an Other beyond humans, an inhuman partner, as it were, best epitomized by the double, by his missing half which is exactly like him and hence all the more irreducible in its otherhood. "*L'enfer, c'est les autres*," ran Sartre's famous quip, "Hell is other people," and one could imagine Beckett's rejoinder "*Le purgatoire, c'est le pseudo-couple*," "Purgatory is the pseudocouple." The double in this couple is never simply a fellow human, he is too close to be the other, an interlocutor and a partner, and because of this closeness all the more the other. There is like an elastic band that holds them together and that they cannot cut, like a semi-cut umbilical cord. There is something mechanical in their relation, a mechanical replication, too mechanical to be plausible or credible, or to be explicable by any psychology, something utterly "improbable" yet uncannily familiar (and Freud took the double precisely as one of the major instances of the uncanny, *das Unheimliche*, the overlap of the same and the other "in one," i.e., "in two"). There is something "more" or something other than selfhood at stake, or the relation between two selves, but without this something "more" or other, there is no self, although this "more" doesn't inhabit anywhere else except the split itself. The doubling points to a real in subjectivity irreducible to the subject. And thus, it is essential not to read into the two the host of oppositions that inevitably spring up and thus endow the two with possible meanings—to endeavor to think, as far as possible, the two as the pure split, the distinction of the indistinct.

I can add an aside. The mere mechanism of a pseudocouple is by itself enough to instigate the comedy setting (like the "forced entertainment," to use Tim Etchells's phrase), the general and pervasive air of hilarity as the underlying tone of the novel, although there might be "nothing funny" in its contents. The double, but in the specific Pascalian sense, is like a machine that unfailingly "fait rire," produces laughter. One might recall that there is a history of the double, or a major historical break affecting its fate, and which pertains precisely to laughter. The pseudocouples were laughed at, they were the major "laughing stock" throughout the comedic tradition, but once the double appeared in the guise of the doppelganger, no one was inclined to laugh. The doppelganger is no laughing matter—it emerged rather suddenly at the end of the eighteenth century, and one can claim that this is an emblematic figure that inaugurated the era of modernity.[49] (By the way, "doppelganger" is one of the very few German words to have made it to the English vocabulary, along with "kindergarten," "sauerkraut," "blitzkrieg," and "berufsverbot." It was first used in English already in 1830.) The very same figure—a couple which is not really a couple, a redoubling of the same—became lethal, the harbinger of death. The doppelganger is not a figure of conflictual non-relation, but the figure of elimination. For the moment the doppelganger appears, the time is up. The world is not big enough for the subject and his double, and the one who is too many, the one who has to go, is the subject. The non-relation is reversed or suspended, the doppelganger is rather the figure of a relation, but an impossible relation that can only be lethal. The double is not pseudo, and hence the relation to it is only possible at the price of death. This entails a powerful script which held in sway the nineteenth century (but which was precisely not an era of comedy). One could maintain that this is one of Beckett's inventions: to reinvent the figure of the pseudocouple for the twentieth century. He had in this one illustrious predecessor for the nineteenth century, Flaubert's *Bouvard et Pécuchet*.—This is an aside that would require a longer elaboration.

*Mercier and Camier* is quite unique in Beckett's oeuvre by the peculiar position of the narrator. The novel starts by the famous entry: "The journey of Mercier and Camier is one I can tell, if I will, for I was with them all the time."[50] Who is the I who speaks and says "I" three times in the first sentence alone? Where is the narrator who was with them all the time, nowhere to be seen, except in every sentence? Later in the novel, he emerges a few times again, his ghost stepping out of the closet:

> Strange impression, said Mercier, strange impression sometimes that we are not alone. You not? / I am not sure I understand, said Camier. / … Like the presence of a third party, said Mercier. Enveloping us. I have felt it from the start. And I am anything but psychic. / Does it bother you? said Camier. / At first no, said Mercier. / And now? said Camier. / It begins to bother me a little, said Mercier.[51]

Another telling passage was omitted for the English translation.

> Let's follow them attentively, Mercier and Camier, let's not move away from them for more than the height of stairs or the thickness of a wall. Let no concern for order or harmony ever make us turn away, for the moment.[52]

The pseudocouple of Mercier and Camier is constantly haunted by the third, inscribing himself invisibly in their midst, following their steps, maybe keeping them together at all. One could read this narratorial instance as a sporadic and ironic reminder of the author, their creator, who can do with them what he wants, they are at his mercy (as Malone and the narrator of *The Unnamable* will never tire of reminding us). He announces from the outset that he can tell this story if he happens to wish so. But maybe one can rather see the narrator as someone who can place himself in the crack between the two, or better, an instance that is enabled and brought about by this crack, the stand-in for the third which is constantly present and invisible, impalpable in the pseudocouple—as if the narrator would lend his voice to what cannot have a voice and cannot be directly presented. This would mean that the narrator is the product, or the function, of the couple, rather than the couple being the product of his fancy and whim (which he ostentatiously asserts in the beginning).

I spent a long time with the pseudocouple as one of the keys to Beckett, and with *Mercier and Camier* as its major embodiment. Let me just add that the vintage embodiment will appear with the two tramps in *Godot*, the one piece that represents Beckett for the zeitgeist (and for the *Halbbildung* of the zeitgeist, in the sense that Adorno has given to that word), reduced to the unfortunate adage

"Godot never comes." So there is the big danger, and a great pity, that this novel is most often read as a proto-Godot, the place where Beckett has discovered his path but is not yet the Beckett who could master it. It is caught in the unhappy spot of "not any more" (the Irish Beckett), "already" (the French Beckett), and "not yet" (the Godot Beckett). But one should at all times try to resist the irresistible charms of the academic obsession with periodization (this is perhaps the discourse of university brought to its gist) and endeavor to reread this novel on its own, by its own standard.[53]

But my intention is rather to present this mechanism of the pseudocouple as a springboard for thinking about other ways, about other Beckettian strategies which can perhaps be seen as an inversion or a transformation of this one—and I am proposing at the end a task that would need much more time to be developed. If one now looks at the *Trilogy*, the problem is set in different, though not unrelated terms. If we set aside *Molloy*, which is based on a very odd pseudocouple of Molloy and Moran, the two narratives mirroring each other, then the problem with *Malone Dies* and *The Unnamable*[54] is rather that the two "narrators" (inadequate word, one should perhaps follow Brian Richardson's proposal to call this *denarration*) don't have their "doubles," they don't have the other, and the problem is precisely how to establish the Other, or rather, whether the Other exists at all.[55] They are caught in their inner universe, the enclosure of their "consciousness," and the existence of another is placed on the very thin line—there is no "inner" without the "external," yet the external vacillates, it keeps evaporating, it is both the "figment of imagination," at the mercy of fancy, and persistently real in its ineradicable fickleness—to the point that the narrator is, in a reversal, at the mercy of the Other which seems to have been merely made up.

> I'll have said it, without a mouth I'll have said it, I'll have said it inside me, then in the same breath outside me, perhaps that's what I feel, an outside and an inside and me in the middle, perhaps that's what I am, the thing that divides the world in two, on the one side the outside, on the other the inside, that can be as thin as foil, I'm neither one side nor the other, I'm in the middle, I'm the partition, I've two surfaces and no thickness, perhaps that's what I feel, myself vibrating, I'm the tympanum, on the one hand the mind, on the other the world, I don't belong to either.[56]

The enunciation is held on that thin line, the very principle of division, itself not on either side, at the intersection of the inner and the outer, but unplaceable in that division, the thinnest of foils which connects and separates the two. The fickleness of consciousness coincides with the fickleness of the "outside," and the outside cannot be positively pinned to any positivity.

This is why the "narrator" constantly endeavors to invent his counterparts, for which Beckett invented another excellent word, another concept, *vice-existers*. The narrator would form a couple with the vice-exister but never manages to come to that. In *The Unnamable* ghosts coming from all previous novels constantly make their appearance, like intruders that won't go away and can't be laid to rest: there are Murphy, Molloy, Malone (the M figures, and perhaps Mercier appears three times because of the M, as opposed to Camier who makes a cameo appearance but once), there is Watt, and then most tellingly Mahood and Worm. This is the reverse side of the pseudocouple logic: the impossibility to form a pseudocouple with the other and the necessity to do so. The vice-existers are but the doubles of the narrator, who is as if looking for his "missing half" and making it up, but not quite, for his own status and "identity" depends on them, they are never just the figures of imagination and fancy, freely made up. Quite the contrary—they are imposing and intruding, they impose the words and the stories on the narrator, it is rather as if the narrator was their invention, the puppet who can only repeat words as received.[57] "The other" may not exist, but it is not therefore merely imaginary; in a reversal it appears more real than the narrator himself. There is a whole vast endeavor to aim at, and seek for, the "real" in it, which presents itself as a commanding presence. Some quotes at random:

> But it's time I gave this solitary a name, nothing doing without proper names. I therefore baptize him Worm. It was high time. Worm. I don't like it, but I haven't much choice. … For if I am Mahood, I am Worm too, plop. Or if I am not yet Worm, I shall be when I cease to be Mahood, plop.[58]

> The essential is never to arrive anywhere, never to be anywhere, neither where Mahood is, nor where Worm is, nor where I am, it little matters thanks to what dispensation.[59]

> Who make me say that since I can't be he I must be he. That since I couldn't be Mahood, as I might have been, I must be Worm, as I cannot be.[60]

What if we were one and the same after all, as he affirms, and I deny?[61]

The impossibility to form a couple, and the constant thrust toward it, is what makes the tenor of these novels. If I proposed the formula "more than one, less than two" for the pseudocouple, then the makeshift formula here would rather be *"less than one, more than two."* The narrator, without the other, without the counterpart, or rather "with without" the counterpart, cannot be one, there is a multiplicity of narratorial voices that he constantly takes up and follows, for his "own" voice is but the thrust of persistence through quoting other voices. And the other, the fickle imagined other, cannot be "one" either, there is a host of characters that flock on that structural place that can never quite get the consistency of oneness. Or shall one say: there is like a couple, but formed of two entities that are in themselves but multiplicities, there is a two, but consisting of two inconsistent entities, whose "ontological" status constantly vacillates, without ever getting to the point of solidity, yet without ever evaporating or dissolving. The impossibility of either of them being counted for one ("less than one") doesn't spill over into the free proliferation of multiplicities (although the narrating voice seems to stray freely wherever the fancy takes it), for they are constantly restrained by repetition and the insistence of impossibility, it's rather like the "infinity" of infinite constraint. At the core of the multiplicities, there is the persistence of the figure of the Two, the impossible couple.

The impossibility to pin down, to delimit, to "ontologically" grasp the One and the Other is played out in two ways: by the mechanism of the pseudocouple in its infinitely protracted non-relation, its neither "with" nor "without," the sheer figure of the two recalcitrant to any whole, flaunting the ineradicable split; or else by the two of the vacillating narrator and his vacillating other who cannot even form this kind of non-relation nor be counted for two. There is a meditation at the bottom on the status of the one, the two, and the multiple, where one cannot conceive either the one or the multiple without the essential figure of the two.

I tried to pin down the two strategies in Beckett's early French work by two handy formulas, "more than one, less than two," and "less than one, more than two." If we look forward to his later work, we can see that the same problem persists, but it develops another, a third strategy that would demand a different further elaboration. In *Comment c'est* (1961, *How It Is*) and in *Le dépeupleur* (1970, *The Lost Ones*) we are dealing with completely "artificial" hermetic universes, worlds constructed on presupposed axioms and rules, but where the essential thrust is the search for a couple, the enforced search, and the couple (if we take *How It Is* as the model) can only be the couple of the henchman and the victim, to the point of the indistinction of the henchman and the victim. This happens in a universe of complete immanence, that is, a universe without the Other, a closed world with no Other and no externality. The couple henchman–victim is thus not in any way sanctioned by the Other, say by the symbolic law and legitimacy, it is purely contingent, depending on the hazard of encounters. So this is the search for the other of the couple in the world devoid of any Other and the contingent formation of couples that lack any support.—I must leave this third strategy as a sketch, a mere designation of something to be developed.

Coming back to the beginning, to Beckett's revelation in 1945, the revelation of the dark as the most precious ally, one can say that the dark was the element of the indistinct, yet misleadingly so insofar as the dark cannot but be caught in the opposition with light (and hence the quasi-dialectic of the reversal of the worst into the best). The proper element was yet to be found, the element of indistinction of dark and light, and hence my title, two shades of gray. Gray is indeed Beckett's proper color—to take just one quote: "Traces fouillis signes sans sens gris pâle presque blanc sur blanc."[62] "Traces blurs light grey almost white on white."[63] Pale gray almost white on white, the dilapidated color, the non-color, strangely evoking Hegel's "grey on grey." "When philosophy paints its grey in grey, then has a shape of life grown old. By philosophy's grey in grey it cannot be rejuvenated but only understood. The owl of Minerva begins its flight only with the falling of dusk."[64] The pure distinction of the indistinct gray, the two shades of gray (no fifty shades of gray, just two shades of gray) with nothing to distinguish them, except for the split, the cut, the minimal "two," at the strange overlap of Beckett[65] and Hegel—this is perhaps a good place to start elaborating our topic of Beckett and dialectics. There is this figure of thought that connects two completely unrelated universes: everything is already finished, it's over, philosophy comes too late, we come too late, always already too late—this is the initial situation of Beckett's novels, this is where they begin. From the first one on—here is the incipit of *Murphy*

(1937): "The sun shone, having no alternative, on the nothing new."⁶⁶ There is no alternative, and there is nothing new under the sun, from the first sentence of the first novel on. How to turn this end into a beginning, a process, a persistence, a loop that opens up however totally restrained we may be by the oppressive reality: this may be seen as Beckett's way to assume Hegel's legacy, to continue Hegel's quote, as it were. "The end is in the beginning, and yet we go on."

# Notes

1. Samuel Beckett, "Krapp's Last Tape," in *The Complete Dramatic Works* (London: Faber and Faber, 1990), 220.

2. Beckett quoted in James Knowlson, *Damned to Fame: The Life of Samuel Beckett* (London: Bloomsbury, 1996), 772. As he also told Knowlson: "Krapp's vision was on the pier at Dún Laoighaire; mine was in my mother's room. Make that clear once and for all." Ibid., 352. So, Beckett was quite adamant about setting the record straight.

3. "*Molloy* and the others came to me the day I became aware of my own folly." Ibid., 352.

4. Samuel Beckett, *Molloy*, ed. Shane Weller (London: Faber and Faber, 2009), 3.

5. Beckett, "Krapp's Last Tape," 220.

6. Beckett quoted in Knowlson, *Damned to Fame*, 352.

7. See Slavoj Žižek, *The Absolute Recoil: Towards a New Foundation of Dialectical Materialism* (London/New York: Verso, 2014), 344–9. "The danger of the catastrophic loss of the essential dimension of being-human also opens up the possibility of a reversal (*Kehre*)." Ibid., 344. Žižek sees this paradigm at work in very different quarters, from Judeo-Christian legacy to Marxism and Heidegger.

8. Beckett was a close reader of Hölderlin, particularly in 1937–8, he held him in very high regard, but precisely as "a failure." There is a fragmented Hölderlin quote at the end of *Watt*. See Dieter Henrich, *Sein oder Nichts: Erkundungen um Samuel Beckett und Hölderlin* (München: C.H.Beck, 2016).

9   Beckett quoted in Knowlson, *Damned to Fame*, 352.

10  Samuel Beckett, "An Interview with Becket," interview by Israel Shenker, in *Samuel Beckett, the Critical Heritage*, ed. Lawrence Graver and Raymond Federman (London/New York: Routledge and Kegan Paul, 1979), 148.

11  Samuel Beckett in a letter to Axel Kaun on July 9, 1937, in *The Letters of Samuel Beckett, Volume I: 1929–1940*, ed. Martha Dow Fehsenfeld and Lois More Overbeck (Cambridge: Cambridge University Press, 2009), 515.

12  Samuel Beckett, "Worstward Ho," in *Company. Ill Seen Ill Said. Worstward Ho. Stirrings Still*, ed. Dirk Van Hulle (London: Faber and Faber, 2009), 95.

13  "… sei es etwas oder nichts…," "be it something or nothing"—doesn't this oscillation point exactly in the direction of Lacan's object a?

14  Beckett quoted in Carlton Lake, ed., *No Symbols Where None Intended* (Austin, TX: Harry Ransom Humanities Research Center, 1948), 49.

15  In a wonderful pun Beckett once said he was writing in French driven by "le besoin d'être mal armé," the need to be poorly equipped as a foreign speaker, but there is Mallarmé lurking behind even the simplest expressions, the most idiomatic of all French poets. Samuel Beckett in a letter to Hans Naumann on February 17, 1954, in *The Letters of Samuel Beckett, Volume II: 1941–1956*, ed. George Craig, Martha Dow Fehsenfeld, Dan Gunn, and Lois More Overbeck (Cambridge: Cambridge University Press, 2011), 462.

16  To be sure, Beckett already tried to write some poetry in French in the late 1930s and participated in an attempted translation of *Watt* into French, and before he started on the novel he wrote two remarkable shorter pieces in French, "La peinture des van Velde ou le monde et le pantalon," and the short story "Suite," with its curious history of publication in *Les temps modernes* (with the subtraction of "la suite," as it were, only the first part having been published), and with its even more curious later renaming to "La fin."

17  For the meticulous comparison between the two "originals" cf. Steven Connor, "Traduttore traditore. Samuel Beckett's Translation of *Mercier et Camier*," *Journal of Beckett Studies* 11–12 (1989): 27–46.

18  Samuel Beckett, *Mercier and Camier*, ed. Seán Kennedy (London: Faber and Faber, 2010), 17.

19  Beckett, *Mercier and Camier*, 16.

20  Cf. Elizabeth Barry, *Beckett and Authority: The Uses of Cliché* (Basingstoke: Palgrave-Macmillan, 2006).

21 Georg Lukács, *The Theory of the Novel: A Historico-philosophical Essay on the Forms of Great Epic Literature*, trans. Anna Bostock (London: Merlin Press, 1971), 73.

22 It may look different for a moment: "The day has dawned at last, after years of shilly-shally, when we must go, we know not whither, perhaps never to return … alive." Beckett, *Mercier and Camier*, 10. (The English translation has "dawn" in it, absent from the French original, thus adding another touch, evoking, and contrasting with, the final dark.) But these are Camier's words to the dim-witted ranger and cannot be taken without the double edge of irony.

23 Samuel Beckett, "Endgame," in *The Complete Dramatic Works* (London: Faber and Faber, 1990), 126.

24 Beckett, *Mercier and Camier*, 101.

25 Samuel Beckett, *Mercier et Camier* (Paris: Les Éditions de Minuit, 1970), 183.

26 Beckett, *Mercier and Camier*, 100.

27 Alain Badiou, "The Writing of the Generic," in *On Beckett*, ed. Nina Power and Alberto Toscano (Manchester: Clinamen Press, 2003), 7.

28 Samuel Beckett, *Malone Dies*, ed. Peter Boxall (London: Faber and Faber, 2009), 52.

29 Cf. Eric P. Levy, "*Mercier and Camier*: Narration, Dante and the Couple," in *On Beckett: Essays and Criticism*, ed. Stanley E. Gontarski (London/New York/Delhi: Anthem Press, 2012), 92–102. The best and most exhaustive book on Beckett's relation to Dante is no doubt Daniela Caselli, *Beckett's Dantes: Intertextuality in the Fiction and Criticism* (Manchester: Manchester University Press, 2005).

30 Beckett, *Mercier and Camier*, 49.

31 "Tu se' lo mio maestro e 'l mio autore; / tu se' solo colui da cu' io tolsi / lo bello stilo che m'ha fatto onore.|" Dante, *Inferno*, 85–7.

32 Beckett, *The Letters Vol. I*, 518.

33 Beckett, *Mercier and Camier*, 31.

34 Ibid., 57.

35 Samuel Beckett, *The Unnamable*, ed. Steven Connor (London: Faber and Faber, 2010), 7.

36 Ibid.

37 Beckett doesn't hyphenate the word in English, as opposed to the French original.

38  For all this cf. the entry "pseudocouples" in Chris J. Ackerley and Stanley E. Gontarski, *The Grove Companion to Samuel Beckett* (New York: Grove Press, 2004), 463–5. The general presence of pseudocouples in Beckett has a tendency to spill over onto his interpreters. Thus one may see Lukács and Adorno, harshly opposed over Beckett, as ultimately a sort of a pseudocouple (cf. Eva Heubach's contribution in the present volume), and throughout the illuminating and meticulous book by Jean-Jacques Lecercle, *Badiou and Deleuze Read Literature* (Edinburgh: Edinburgh University Press, 2010), it appears that Badiou and Deleuze feature as a pseudocouple.

39  Beckett, *Mercier and Camier*, 50.

40  Alain Badiou, "Tireless Desire," in *On Beckett*, ed. Nina Power and Alberto Toscano (Manchester: Clinamen Press, 2003), 42.

41  Cf. the classical reference in Ovid: "Sic ego nec sine te nec tecum vivere possum." "Thus I cannot live either without you or with you." Ovid, *Amores* III, ix, 39.

42  Peter Boxall, ed., *Samuel Beckett—Waiting for Godot/Endgame: A Reader's Guide to Essential Criticism* (Basingstoke: Palgrave Macmillan, 2000), 32.

43  Samuel Beckett, *Watt*, ed. Chris J. Ackerley (London: Faber and Faber, 2009), 221.

44  Ibid., 222.

45  For all this see the entry "hardy laurel" in Ackerley and Gontarski, *The Grove Companion to Samuel Beckett*, 246.

46  Beckett, *Mercier and Camier*, 92.

47  Ibid., 38.

48  Blaise Pascal, *Pascal's Pensées*, with an Introduction by T. S. Eliot (New York: E. P. Dutton & Co., 1958), 67. "Deux visages semblables, dont aucun ne fait rire en particulier, font rire ensemble par leur ressemblance." Blaise Pascal, *Pensées*, ed. Philippe Sellier and Gérard Ferreyrolles (Paris: Le livre de poche, 2000), 58. Jean Anouilh, in a famous quip, once said that *Godot* was like "Pascal's *Pensées* arranged into sketch and acted by the Fratellini Brothers" ("un sketch de Pensée de Pascal traité par les Fratellini"). Actually, the remark is more to the point than Anouilh might have imagined, for the Fratellini Brothers are not an external imposition on *Pensées*, but already inscribed in them, a device foreseen and brought to concept by Pascal himself.

49  It appears that the expression, "der Doppelgänger," was first employed by Jean Paul in *Siebenkäs* in 1796, and this first occurrence was soon followed by an avalanche. It is no coincidence that the first elaboration of the theme of the doppelganger was made by Jean Paul as a sort of parody of Fichte,

the modern grounding of the "absolute I" immediately in the tracks of the French revolution. The doppelganger is the absolute other of the absolute I precisely by being the same. It is but a phantom, it is not an existing entity, it is not an object of knowledge or possible cognition, but hence all-powerful, intruding precisely at the point where the "absolute I" seemed to be the absolute master, the flip side of the modern subject.

50   Beckett, *Mercier and Camier*, 3.

51   Ibid., 83.

52   Beckett, *Mercier et Camier*, 96 [my clumsy translation].

53   Perhaps the best antidote against this proclivity for periodization was given by the Slovene group Laibach in an interview: "Our development went through three phases: the first one, the second one and the third one."

54   Badiou's catchy title *De quoi Sarkozy est-il le nom?* (Paris: Lignes, 2007), gave rise to countless variations, but the best one could actually be *De quoi l'innommable est-il le nom?* What is the unnamable the name of?

55   Cf. Brian Richardson, "Denarration in Fiction: Erasing the Story in Beckett and Others," *Narrative* 9, no. 2 (May 2001): 168–75.

56   Beckett, *The Unnamable*, 100.

57   "I shall transmit the words as received, by the ear, or roared through a trumpet into the arsehole, in all their purity, and in the same order, as far as possible. This infinitesimal lag, between arrival and departure, this trifling delay in evacuation, is all I have to worry about." Ibid., 63.

58   Ibid., 51.

59   Ibid., 52.

60   Ibid., 61.

61   Ibid., 26.

62   Samuel Beckett, *Têtes-Mortes* (Paris: Les Éditions de Minuit, 1992), 62.

63   Samuel Beckett, "Ping," in *The Complete Short Prose: 1929–1989*, ed. Stanley E. Gontarski (New York: Grove Press, 1995), 193.

64   Georg Wilhelm Friedrich Hegel, *Outlines of the Philosophy of Right*, trans. Thomas Malcolm Knox (Oxford: Oxford University Press, 2008), 16.

65   When Beckett was asked whether he had any wishes as to the color of his gravestone, he said, "I don't mind as long as it's grey."

66   Samuel Beckett, *Murphy*, ed. James C. C. Mays (London: Faber and Faber, 2009), 3.

# Bibliography

Ackerley, Chris J., and Stanley E. Gontarski. *The Grove Companion to Samuel Beckett*. New York: Grove Press, 2004.

Badiou, Alain. "Tireless Desire." In *On Beckett*, edited by Nina Power and Alberto Toscano, 37–78. Manchester: Clinamen Press, 2003.

Badiou, Alain. "The Writing of the Generic." In *On Beckett*, edited by Nina Power and Alberto Toscano, 1–36. Manchester: Clinamen Press, 2003.

Badiou, Alain. *De quoi Sarkozy est-il le nom?* Paris: Lignes, 2007.

Barry, Elizabeth. *Beckett and Authority: The Uses of Cliché*. Basingstoke: Palgrave-Macmillan, 2006.

Beckett, Samuel. *Mercier et Camier*. Paris: Les Éditions de Minuit, 1970.

Beckett, Samuel. "An Interview with Becket." Interview by Israel Shenker. In *Samuel Beckett, the Critical Heritage*, edited by Lawrence Graver and Raymond Federman, 146–8. London/New York: Routledge and Kegan Paul, 1979.

Beckett, Samuel. "Endgame." In *The Complete Dramatic Works*, 89–134. London: Faber and Faber, 1990.

Beckett, Samuel. "Krapp's Last Tape." In *The Complete Dramatic Works*, 213–23. London: Faber and Faber, 1990.

Beckett, Samuel. *Têtes Mortes*. Paris: Les Éditions de Minuit, 1992.

Beckett, Samuel. "Ping." In *The Complete Short Prose: 1929–1989*, edited by Stanley E. Gontarski, 193–6. New York: Grove Press, 1995.

Beckett, Samuel. *The Letters of Samuel Beckett, Volume I: 1929–1940*, edited by Martha Dow Fehsenfeld and Lois More Overbeck. Cambridge: Cambridge University Press, 2009.

Beckett, Samuel. *Molloy*, edited by Shane Weller. London: Faber and Faber, 2009.

Beckett, Samuel. *Murphy*, edited by James C. C. Mays. London: Faber and Faber, 2009.

Beckett, Samuel. *Watt*, edited by Chris J. Ackerley. London: Faber and Faber, 2009.

Beckett, Samuel. "Worstward Ho." In *Company. Ill Seen Ill Said. Worstward Ho. Stirrings Still*, edited by Dirk Van Hulle, 79–103. London: Faber and Faber, 2009.

Beckett, Samuel. *Malone Dies*, edited by Peter Boxall. London: Faber and Faber, 2010.

Beckett, Samuel. *Mercier and Camier*, edited by Seán Kennedy. London: Faber and Faber, 2010.

Beckett, Samuel. *The Unnamable*, edited by Steven Connor. London: Faber and Faber, 2010.

Beckett, Samuel. *The Letters of Samuel Beckett, Volume II: 1941–1956*, edited by George Craig, Martha Dow Fehsenfeld, Dan Gunn, and Lois More Overbeck. Cambridge: Cambridge University Press, 2011.

Boxall, Peter, ed. *Samuel Beckett—Waiting for Godot/Endgame: A Reader's Guide to Essential Criticism*. Basingstoke: Palgrave Macmillan, 2000.

Caselli, Daniela. *Beckett's Dantes: Intertextuality in the Fiction and Criticism*. Manchester: Manchester University Press, 2005.

Connor, Steven. "Traduttore traditore. Samuel Beckett's Translation of *Mercier et Camier*." *Journal of Beckett Studies* 11–12 (1989): 27–46.

Hegel, Georg Wilhelm Friedrich. *Outlines of the Philosophy of Right*, translated by T. M. Knox. Oxford: Oxford University Press, 2008.

Henrich, Dieter. *Sein oder Nichts: Erkundungen um Samuel Beckett und Hölderlin*. München: C.H. Beck, 2016.

Knowlson, James. *Damned to Fame: The Life of Samuel Beckett*. London: Bloomsbury, 1996.

Lake, Carlton, ed. *No Symbols Where None Intended*. Austin, TX: Harry Ransom Humanities Research Center, 1984.

Lecercle, Jean-Jacques. *Badiou and Deleuze Read Literature*. Edinburgh: Edinburgh University Press, 2010.

Levy, Eric. "Mercier and Camier: Narration, Dante and the Couple." In *On Beckett: Essays and Criticism*, edited by Stanley E. Gontarski, 92–102. London/New York/Delhi: Anthem Press, 2012.

Lukács, Georg. *The Theory of the Novel: A Historico-Philosophical Essay on the Forms of Great Epic Literature*, translated by Anna Bostock. London: Merlin Press, 1971.

Pascal, Blaise. *Pascal's Pensées*. With an Introduction by T. S. Eliot. New York: E. P. Dutton & Co., 1958.

Pascal, Blaise. *Pensées*, edited by Philippe Sellier and Gérard Ferreyrolles. Paris: Le livre de poche, 2000.

Richardson, Brian. "Denarration in Fiction: Erasing the Story in Beckett and Others." *Narrative* 9, no. 2 (May 2001): 168–75.

Žižek, Slavoj. *The Absolute Recoil: Towards a New Foundation of Dialectical Materialism*. London/New York: Verso, 2014.

# IV

# Senile Dialectic

## Rebecca Comay

Efforts to read Beckett with (or against) Hegel sometimes present Beckett as an anti-Hegel, a Hegel-in-reverse: not exactly flipped back onto his feet, as Marx attempted, but experimenting with a more challenging maneuver—limping or crawling backward, collapsing downward, going under, falling, shuffling, slithering nowhere, shrinking, getting poorer, weaker, thinner, smaller—forever worstward to Hegel's westward, ever the pessimist to Hegel's optimist, forever the anorexic to Hegel's bulimic, always less to Hegel's more. It is tempting to graft this opposition between increase and decrease, between encyclopedic expansion and minimalist contraction onto the standard account—that is to say, Beckett's own account—of the Joyce-Beckett pseudocouple: "The more Joyce knew the more he could. He's tending toward omniscience and omnipotence as an artist. I'm working with impotence, ignorance."[1] Alternatively, which probably amounts to the same thing, Beckett sometimes figures as a kind of hyper-Hegelian—maestro of failure, master of the dialectical salvage, finding success in defeat, gleaning from the extremity of destitution an inverted index of redemption. Slavoj Žižek describes this reverse teleology, which, when you think about it, turns out to be just regular teleology, as the "Hölderlin paradigm" (a trope Mladen Dolar has also recently troubled): where the danger lurks, there grows the saving power ….[2] Adorno can sometimes come unfortunately close to this sort of negative eschatology.

I'm going to try something different. Maybe we're looking through the wrong end of the telescope. Instead of looking for Hegel in Beckett, perhaps it's time to turn the tables. Rather than trying to flush out the dialectic in the drama, maybe we should start exploring the drama of the dialectic. What would happen if we tried to Beckettize Hegel? Or better yet: what if Hegel himself *were* Beckett? In other words: How are we to read Hegel today? This is, of course, a perfectly ordinary Hegelian question.

## Gray Canon

Hegel doesn't occupy a huge place in the "gray canon" of Beckettiana—the ever-growing penumbra of unpublished writings, drafts, theater notebooks, diaries, letters, gnomic pronouncements.[3] Philosophy occupies a peculiar place in this shadow canon. Beckett was famously skittish about philosophical approaches to his work even as he incited them. *No symbols where none intended.*[4] He claimed to be "not unduly concerned with intelligibility,"[5] studiously refusing to comment when asked to explain things or to supply allegorical meanings or morals. *If people want to have headaches among the overtones, let them. And provide their own aspirin.*[6] These nuggets of recalcitrance, together with the fond anecdotes encasing them, are among the most cherished treasures of the archive.[7] Beckett's mulishness, of course, makes him even more adorable to philosophers, who always enjoy being told off by real writers; it gives them a chance to talk about the philosophy–literature divide; they get to act humble for a minute; they get to flatter themselves for their ineptness; it gives them a free pass to say whatever they were going to say anyway.

Beckett was not being entirely disingenuous when he insisted he had read no philosophy, that he was not a philosopher, that he understood nothing about philosophy, but he was not exactly telling the whole truth either.[8] It is perhaps technically the case he had *read* little philosophy, in the sense of having gone the extra mile and actually slogged through a ton of primary sources. People have tracked the marginalia in Beckett's personal library. They've measured the dog-eared pages—it seems that he had a special technique of folding down corners, so that even with his second-hand books the experts can tell you exactly which pages he paused at—and all things considered the evidence is scanty.[9] But Beckett had definitely read all *about* philosophy, having tunneled his way through basically the entire history of Western philosophy or what passed for that *c.* 1930. Curiously, Beckett consumed almost all his philosophy second-hand through a scrim of text-books and surveys; after narrowly escaping a career in academia, he spent countless hours in libraries in Dublin and London diligently going through the prescribed reading list of the undergraduate philosophy curriculum of Trinity College Dublin.[10] The "Philosophy Notes," compiled over several years during the early 1930s—the purgatorial interlude between Beckett's life as an academic and his life as an artist—fill almost 300 densely written pages and cover the history of Western philosophy from Thales to Nietzsche.[11] The bulk of the notes are taken from the English translation of Wilhelm Windelband's massive *History of Philosophy*.[12] The philosophy notes were found stashed with other notebooks in a cellar years after Beckett's death, about a thousand pages in total, everything packed up in brown paper like an offering from beyond the grave, already classified and catalogue-ready, neatly labeled in Beckett's handwriting: "Notes diverse holo."[13] (Holo., as in, holograph: this is a dead man speaking; does anybody actually use this word, apart from archivists and rare book sellers?)

This is a strange thing to be doing with your newfound freedom.[14]

I spent several days in the Beckett collection at Trinity College library last summer quietly going mad as I struggled to decipher his unreadable handwriting. Beckett had filled virtually every page with paragraphs and sometimes entire pages copied verbatim from Windelband's *History*, including the table of contents and footnotes. His transcriptions were so faithful that I would often find myself consulting Windelband to supply a word when Beckett's writing got too illegible or I got impatient. There was barely a word of commentary or analysis. From time to time a little gesture would break up the monotony like a shaft of sunshine piercing through the gray Dublin sky—a blotch, a doodle, a change of pen, a nod or grimace. Things got a bit livelier when I reached the home stretch on modern German philosophy. When Beckett gets to the Categorical Imperative (which he nicknames the "C.I."), he writes in the margins: "But what the G.L. [i.e., "Good Lord"] *are* the maxims?"[15] He describes Schopenhauer's universe as a "ball aching world." Of Schlegel all he has to say is "pfui!"[16]

I would stagger out at the end of the day blinded from hours of staring at wobbly microfilm (the physical notebooks were out of bounds, the microfilm itself was under lock and key, and printouts were prohibited by order of the estate, all of which managed to generate a faint aura; it made me vaguely nostalgic for the pre-internet days when you could still justify making scholarly pilgrimages across the ocean and didn't have to feel so guilty about air travel). Hunched over the antiquated machine, hearing the clatter and whir of celluloid as it passed from one spool to another, I entertained myself by fast-forwarding and reversing, pretending to be Krapp, but mostly it was unrelieved boredom. I'd been secretly hoping that I'd be doing this under the vaulted ceiling of the Long Room in the Old Library, where Beckett himself had passed so many diligent hours, sitting like a monk in a scriptorium amidst the manuscripts and rare books, but that was not to be. That splendorous space was off limits except to the crowds of tourists lining up for the Book of Kells. Unsure what I was looking for, and feeling idiotic, I found myself transcribing passages of Beckett's transcripts in my own little notebook as if the repetition might somehow ignite a spark, like rubbing flints together. Headaches among the overtones without the overtones.

I wondered what it felt like to have escaped the "loutishness of learning" (Beckett's summation of the academic rigmarole) only to end up shackled to a desk copying out the textbook in preparation for the final exam.[17] There was something oddly self-punishing, I am tempted to say Beckettian, in the thought of Beckett spending all those hours sitting in a library blindly copying. I thought of the Autodidact in *La Nausée*. (Beckett loved that novel. He didn't especially approve of the existentialist feeding frenzy generated by his own works, but he admired this one; he found it "extraordinarily good."[18]) I thought of Bouvard and Pécuchet, accessorized like Didi and Gogo with their matching bowler hats, how they had quit their day jobs to start their new life in the country, only to find out that the life of retirement was nothing more than an unpaid research leave—a life sentence of endless reading lists, book orders, a growing heap of unmanageable assignments, more topics to fail to master, more broken off investigations, more impasses and clashing theories, a nightmare of interminable preparation. Even suicide proved not to be an option for these two because they hadn't gotten around to doing the necessary paperwork. I thought of Flaubert doing his own "research" in preparation for *Bouvard et Pécuchet*, the supposed 1,500 books and articles that he felt he needed to get through before starting to write the novel that he would never finish, his *physical* need to keep copying and recopying his sources, his avowed preference for second-rate materials, the almost photographic exactitude of his literalism. I thought about the paradoxical austerity driving Flaubert's binge-reading, the peculiar minimalism he managed to forge from a lifetime of unrestrained bibliographic foraging. Here's the secret of Flaubert's docta ignorantia: you must *learn* how to be stupid to show the stupidity of learning.

I thought, of course, of Bartleby.

I took a break. I decided I needed a new pen. I accidentally ended up on a discussion-board for aficionados of expensive fountain pens, where I stumbled on a little trouvaille from the margins of a discarded manuscript of *Murphy*: "What is my life, but the preference for the ginger nut biscuit?"[19]

I thought of Auguste Blanqui, the revolutionary conspirator, locked up in his prison cell in Fort Taureau, hallucinating his demonic vision of the eternal return while the Paris Commune burned. After three failed revolutions—perhaps four, depending on how you're counting, if you're still counting—it went like this: "The same drama, the same setting, on the same narrow stage … the same monotony, the same immobility … The universe repeats itself endlessly and paws the ground in place …"[20] Walter Benjamin took this to be the definition of myth: a schoolchild's punishment—*die Strafe des Nachsitzens*, life as a never-ending detention. "Humanity has to keep on copying out the same text, again and again, forever."[21]

While Beckett was sitting in the reading room of the British Museum copying out Windelband, Benjamin was sitting in the reading room of the Bibliothèque Nationale in Paris copying out just about everything in sight—collecting, sorting, filing, recopying, splicing, cross-indexing, color-coding, obsessively assembling and reassembling the heaps of quotations that would overflow the bursting folders of the *Arcades Project*. In a letter to Gershom Scholem, he described his unfinished, unfinishable project as the "theater of all my struggles and all my ideas."[22] As the piles of notes mounted, Benjamin started fantasizing about scrapping the original project for which this was supposedly to be the research; he dreamed of writing a book that would consist of nothing but quotations.

I thought of the scenes of force-feeding and elimination in the *Unnamable*. I thought about the scenes of torture and forced confession in *How It Is*.[23] I thought about Clov and Hamm trapped in the theater night after night repeating each other's lines—"All life long the same questions, the same answers"[24]—while Nagg and Nell tease and torment each other with their half-remembered jokes and anecdotes. I thought of the Latin-spouting parrot in *Malone Dies*. I thought about Lucky's brain exploding like a grenade under the pressure of all that cramming.

I thought about the unhappy consciousness in Hegel's *Phenomenology*. Imagine the plight: a subject bereft of all coordinates, marooned in longing for a nonexistent object, driven to the abyss of idiocy—submitting to the automatism of empty ritual, reciting formulas it does not understand, in a language it does not know. Hegel, being himself, manages to turn everything around at zero hour: it turns out that stupidity can wondrously clear the mind. In submitting to the force of repetition—reducing language to the regurgitation of empty phrases, divesting words of their significance—I purge myself of the last dregs of stubborn particularity and close the gap separating me from the elusive object of my desire.[25] I become a machine and thereby win my humanity. In losing myself, I reclaim the world … et voilà … the birth of Reason from the ashes of unreason. (Hegel is talking about the rituals of

Catholicism, which may seem like a back-handed compliment, but he means it sincerely.)

I thought about the five minutes of sunshine on St Stephen's Green, about how I had used up all this research money, and about what I would say when I got home and my colleagues asked me what had I been "working on" this summer …

Hegel barely figures in the "Philosophy Notebooks," which is both astonishing and understandable. Understandable, given Beckett's sources. Windelband was an influential neo-Kantian, co-founder of the Baden school, although his approach is avowedly heterodox ("to understand Kant means to go beyond him"). Even to be undertaking a *History of Philosophy* of this scope and magnitude is notable for a self-respecting Kantian, and Windelband's account of post-Kantian idealism is relatively evenhanded and expansive. But astounding nonetheless. Beckett's notes on Hegel take up less than one page.[26] There will be no further references to Hegel, not even after the war when Beckett has settled permanently in Paris and Hegel is everywhere in the air. He seems to have been untouched and incurious about the excitement generated by Kojève's lectures in the 1930s.[27] While Beckett was slaving away over Windelband in the Trinity College Library, all of Paris had been thrumming to the beat of the Master–Slave.

## No More Nature

Some readers try to apply the Master–Slave dialectic to the parade of dysfunctional couples (Beckett speaks of "pseudocouples") populating the Beckett universe—Hamm and Clov, Mercier and Camier, Winnie and Willie, Didi and Gogo, Molloy and Moran—all these inseparable pairs chained together, rotating around each other, swapping lines, inciting and ignoring each other, shadowing and obstructing each other in the murky zone of indistinction, the gray zone where the line between oppressed and oppressor, victim and perpetrator, keeps blurring. *Nec tecum nec sine te* ....[28] There are many reasons why the Master–Slave paradigm doesn't quite work in Beckett. For starters, *nothing* in Beckett quite works—nobody and nothing is working, nothing is getting done, nothing is being produced, there is no making or self-making, no project or prospect of *Bildung*, no significant act that would signal the subject's singular or collective entry upon the stage of history, no occasion for spiritual development, maturation, discovery, insight. The roast chicken appears from nowhere. The inoperativity goes all the way down.

"*There is no more nature.*"[29] It's not just that nature has run out, along with bicycle wheels and painkillers, that it has become another commodity to be measured and meted out, a stock that depletes, a machine that breaks down (even the sun doesn't really set, in Beckett, it goes to zero, it switches off, it goes *kaput*). The more devastating point is that there never *was* a Nature—there is no primal plenitude to puncture or plunder, no originary unity to lose and recover, no immediacy from which to affirm or lament my distance. There is no more Nature and therefore there can be no more Spirit. There is no backdrop against which to prove my human mettle, no animal appetite against which to assert the dignity of my own desire, no ground on which to trace the figure of my freedom, no substance in which to lose and retrieve myself as subject—this means: no sacrifice, no heroism, no sovereign decision. This also means: no more staring into the abyss to see my own monstrosity reflected. We should relinquish the guilty but ultimately self-exculpating and self-aggrandizing fantasy that "we" (homo sapiens) have ruined the planet through our collective hubris. We should give up the consoling fantasy that there is a universal subject of history who bears responsibility for the disaster as if the guilt were shared generically and the costs evenly distributed; we should purge the obfuscating tag "Anthropocene" from our lexicon. It's not Man who carved his name into the earth. In short: there can be no viable relation to the environment without a global transformation of all social relations. (This may be more than Beckett is holding out for. "You're on earth. There's no cure for that.")

That there is no more nature means that there is no life to stake, that there is nothing at stake, that there is no more struggle to the death, that dying itself is impossible and redundant—impossible precisely *because* it is redundant, redundant because it has already occurred. There is no death because there is no life, because life does not live. "Death, the absolute master" loses its grandeur and the scene of sovereignty dissolves. This means that recognition ceases to be the gold standard of ethical and social life. I'll come back to this in a minute.

This undermines the minimal conditions of theater. The celebrated face-off between Master and Slave is a "primal scene" in more than one sense. It is *primal,* in that it is the first time in the narrative of the *Phenomenology* that consciousness explicitly confronts its inherent sociability. Spirit from here on in is explicitly issued in n+1 editions; it lives in a world of mirrors and doubles; it henceforth marches on stage two by two like the animals entering Noah's ark: Lord and Bondsman, Antigone and Creon, Wealth and Power, Base and Noble, Faith and Insight …. To say that consciousness must from now on partner up, that its solitary Cartesian days are over, is not to say that it will hook up willingly or even knowingly, that it will find an appropriate dance-partner, or that it feels it needs one. The remainder of the *Phenomenology* will be the tireless saga of doomed relationships and futile attempts to flee them.

But this primal scene is also a *scene*: it establishes the primacy of the stage as the fundamental locus of self-consciousness. In putting my life at stake, in needing to show that I am more than nature, I have already shown that I am more than nature. The *need* to prove myself, to put on a show, is the very proof I'm seeking. The desire to exit nature is itself already an unnatural desire: all desire is in this sense profoundly self-ratifying, which is another way of saying that desire is the desire to desire. Freedom *is* theater. It is an act that displays itself as act: not only do I act but I must act as if I'm acting; I act like an actor; I show that I can act; I show others how to act; I show what acting and action really are. In acting, I make a claim for action and I define the terms of human action. But it is theater too that is being put on trial: every act is also an experiment in dramaturgical theory and practice, a testing of the conditions, and protocols of performance.

This introduces the seed of doubt that my act might be just that—an act, a performance, a fiction, a fakery; naturally, I'm the first to fall for my own duplicity, while the "non-dupes err" in their efforts to expose it.³⁰ The twists and turns of the *Phenomenology* all uncoil from this fundamental uncertainty; everything that happens or fails to happen takes place at the porous border between semblance and dissemblance. Experience is the anxious skittering along the shifting fault line between the self-evident and the (merely) apparent—the endless shuttle between truth and certainty, between essence and appearance. But all this double-dealing and second-guessing presupposes that there *is* a nature to transcend, that there is something to prove and someone to whom to prove it, that there is a witness, even if only to witness my demand for witness, and to ratify the—irreducibly historical, contested, shifting—protocols of evidence and testimony. Without this minimum condition, the theater of appearances, and phenomenology itself, dissolves.

Beckett retracts even this minimal condition. All that is left is "the dialogue"³¹ (as Hamm calls it, for lack of a better word)—the need to keep on talking, the inability to sit quietly in a room, the need to keep on going.

Finally the master–slave encounter is a *primal scene* in the Freudian sense: it acquires its primacy, it becomes inaugural, paradigmatic, and foundational, only retroactively in the light of its subsequent re-stagings. I'm talking about more than just the perspicacity of hindsight. The scene *becomes* primal only belatedly through the incidents and accidents that follow. It becomes earlier later. For better and worse, the Master–Slave will become the origin myth for the history of Spirit and the key to its narrative unfolding, the prize exemplar of the dialectic in its glory; every subsequent episode in the *Phenomenology*, and Hegel's entire project, and modernity itself, will come to be understood as a protracted "struggle for recognition." This is why the episode will inspire such generative misreadings—a paean to freedom, a call to action, a vindication of the workers' struggle, an allegory of rebellion, a tale of erotic bondage, an oblique reflection of the Haitian slave revolution. I say misreadings, but I do not mean this disparagingly, just that if I were to take Hegel at his word, the Master–Slave chapter is about the last place I'd go looking for revolutionary inspiration.[32]

That this episode has acquired its canonical stature is at least in part a function of the reader's craving for a gripping narrative beginning—a starting point memorable enough to provide direction and guidance for the labyrinthine tale that follows. But its prestige is also a function of the humanist framework that shaped the interwar reception of Hegel and continues to this day. A version of this humanism informs most contemporary (largely liberal and largely defanged) readings of Hegel that persist in seeing him as a theorist of recognition. What these readings take for granted, or do not fully question, are the idealist premises of Hegel's argument—namely, the Nature–Spirit dichotomy that seems to frame and organize his system as a whole. This dichotomy between human and nonhuman nature invariably reproduces itself as the (racialized and gendered) dichotomy within humanity itself, between the human and the not-really or not-yet human; Hegel's manifest Eurocentrism and misogyny are ultimately rooted in this dichotomy. Spirit emerges, and must prove itself, as the sacrifice or self-cancellation of non-human or less-than-fully-human Nature. To be human you need to demonstrate your own humanity. This performance requires visible and invisible procedures of exclusion, policing, coercion. In short: theater is an institution and institutions have protocols. Within the limits of this framework, it is unsurprising that freedom is so often construed in *humanitarian* terms as a demand for inclusion—a claim to acknowledgment or recognition. But there are other ways to think about freedom.

Here's another way of putting it. In Hegel, every relationship—every quarrel, every struggle, every standoff—is embedded within a larger intersubjective context. There is a symbolic order grounding and accounting for every impasse and providing an implicit horizon of recognition. Every shape of spirit thus appears as a miniaturized dramaticule contained within a larger drama—it "comes on the scene" as an abridged theatrical performance, a set-piece inscribed within a larger dramatic arc. The succession of chapters in the *Phenomenology* can be read as a sequence of mini-tragedies—rise and fall, peripeteia and anagnorisis, catastrophe and catharsis—stitched into a larger *commedia* of redemption. That the whole thing eventually implodes, that the climax turns out to be an underwhelming anticlimax, only underscores the force of the organizing fantasy and reveals our stubborn attachment to the magical power of narrative closure and our unquenchable desire for a Master—a subject-supposed-to-know—who controls the story and possesses the key to its interpretation. (Hegel himself encourages this fantasy at the beginning of the *Phenomenology* when he requests the reader's trust and dangles the promise of eventual resolution.)

The ending of the *Phenomenology* explodes this fantasy. The final chapter on Absolute Knowing turns out to be a potted (and not entirely accurate) summary of the preceding seven chapters delivered at breakneck speed—Windelband lite. Our sense of deflation only betrays our childish investment in a good ending and proves that we really weren't understanding what we'd been reading all this time anyway.[33] Dorothy reaches the Emerald City only to discover, when she finally lifts the curtain, that the Wizard of Oz is just another middle-aged man playing with his gadgets. The Master is too busy writing out his lecture notes to talk to us. We attain the peaks of Mount Olympus only to discover that the ether we've been seeking is just the air we've been breathing all along. The Absolute was already with us from the start. We're still in Kansas.

In Beckett, in contrast, the fantasy never even gets off the ground. This is because the torture chamber is sealed. Even the *fantasy* of an exterior vantage point is unsustainable and only half-heartedly engaged. The players are suspended in an abstract theatrical space—trapped in a room, locked in cylinders, stuck in urns or garbage cans, confined in windowless interiors,[34] or aimlessly circling around each other in an unmarked landscape. This makes for peculiar theater.[35] Every episode is sealed off and disconnected not only from every other episode but from any possible spectator. It's not exactly that there is a fourth wall separating the viewers from the actors, although Beckett will never relinquish the convention of the proscenium stage.[36] It's rather that we are barred from occupying *any* spectatorial position in the "very closed box" of Beckett's theater.[37] The problem with the fourth wall is that it is actually a window. It produces an illusionistic spectacle powerful enough to incite our voyeurism and enable our absorption: in removing us from the scene, the fourth wall seduces us and draws us in. Beckett simultaneously tears down the fourth wall and builds it thicker. We are forcibly inserted into a scene from which we are denied access. Even while trapped within the confined space of Beckett's theater implicated and without alibi, we are barred from occupying either a spectatorial or a participatory position.

This is because there is no symbolic order, not even the fantasy of a big Other organizing, explicating, and observing (and, by this token, providing an imaginary vantage point that would enable ourselves to witness) the stand-off. This is true even where the relationship seems to be orchestrated from the outside (e.g., by the remote power of Youdi, in *Molloy*); even where language is explicitly registered as an impersonal system imposed or extorted from without (as with the language torture inflicted on the Unnamable or in *How It Is*); or even where surveillance is foregrounded by the onstage presence of Auditors, Directors, and Stenographers, or by a panoply of monitoring devices (chronometers, thermometers, barometers, hygrometers, telescopes, tape recorders, etc.). The manic calculation running throughout Beckett's corpus—Murphy's 1.83 cups of tea; Molloy's algorithm for the sucking stones; the Speaker's computation, in *A Piece of Monologue*, of the total number of seconds in a normal lifetime (answer, if you're wondering: two and a half billion); the mathematical speculations in *Watt* and *How It Is;* the counting of footsteps in *Footfalls*—all this frenetic measurement underscores the basic absence of measure in a world in which man no longer supplies the measure. I'll come back to this.

## Senile, demented dialectic

In his *Aesthetic Theory*, Adorno describes the logic of *Godot*, and by extension Beckett generally, as a "senile and demented dialectic."[38] This sounds right to me, and not only for the reasons Adorno offers. Adorno is referring to the persistence of archaic relations of domination in an age when scarcity has or should have been eliminated; he is thinking specifically about Pozzo's cruelty—the surplus of violence even in the exercise of (overt) economic coercion. Such unembellished violence appears in one of its starkest forms when a regime generates artificial scarcities to sustain its power. The artificially induced Irish famine ("starvation in the midst of plenty") is a case in point, the echoes of which haunt Beckett's corpus, as James McNaughton and others have shown.[39] In another register, we can observe the insistent return of "ancient voices" within the confined spaces of the modern interior (office, interrogation chamber, prison)—for example, the recycling of Sadean protocols within the contemporary-sounding torture scenes of *How It Is* and *What Where*. (These latter texts stage an anachronism within an anachronism: Sade's rituals were themselves already an untimely hybrid of new–old procedures, a grafting of courtly etiquette with modern disciplinary practices.)

We can think about this persistence as a kind of formal subsumption in Marx's sense, where historically outdated remnants linger on beyond their expiration date and are absorbed by capitalism without having been either transformed or integrated. These atavistic leftovers are "subsumed" without being metabolized, producing a wrinkle of untimeliness within the homogeneous continuum of time. Modernity requires this non-synchronicity for its own maintenance and self-presence; it needs the tug of anachronism to sustain its own forward momentum.

At a formal level, this senility is expressed as the lingering persistence of obsolete literary tropes—what Adorno describes as the persistence of tragic form "in the age of its impossibility."[40] Numerous reasons for this impossibility have been offered from opposite ends of the political spectrum, and Adorno gives several of his own, noting how the smattered remnants of tragedy recombine and recirculate as cultural trash. He draws particular attention to Beckett's exaggerated observance of the tragic unities: the unity of time is parodied as the day where the interval between the rising and the setting of the sun collapses; the unity of place is parodied as the shrunken space of the cell; the unity of action is parodied as the inane repetition of inaction.

But the idea of senility is evocative in other ways as well. It captures the strange tempo and rhythms of Beckett's language—the convergence of persistence and dissolution, fixity and interruption, persistence and evanescence. We might describe this as a kind of "petrified unrest" (to push Benjamin's oxymoron in a non-Benjaminian direction). The whole thing has a geriatric feel: on the one hand, obstinacy, rumination, aimless perseveration; on the other hand, fluctuation, dissipation, distraction. It plays out as the incessant reiteration of half-finished thoughts and phrases, as the endless recitation of garbled anecdotes and cultural allusions. And it underscores the paradox of all repetition. Repetition betrays a simultaneous excess and deficiency of memory: it expresses at once forgetfulness and the impossibility of forgetting. One cannot forget what one cannot remember, so everything keeps recurring but always as if for the first time. We over-remember precisely because we cannot remember, because it is impossible to "revolve it all," and so the past keeps coming back unmodified and unmetabolized with its shock value unabated.[41]

This puts a new twist on the self-referential conundrums that for so many decades tormented and entertained the post-Hegelian aftermath—the seeming impossibility of contesting, resisting, exceeding, getting out of, going on from, going after, getting away from Hegel, breaking out of his orbit, or even saying where exactly the problem lies. What would it take to *overcome* Hegel, to move beyond the elevating powers of the *Aufhebung*? To *overturn* or *overthrow* Hegel, to *invert* the speculative inversion? Can one *negate* the negative—negativity—without performing another negation of the negation? Is there an *opposition* to dialectic that does not take the form of a dialectical opposition? Deliberately or not, Nietzsche formalizes the problem trenchantly in *Ecce Homo*: "I contradict myself but I am the opposite of a nay-saying spirit."[42] Is there a *critique* of the Hegelian system that does not involve a basic commitment to this system, or at least share his grandiose faith in system generally? (There is no such thing as piecemeal critique; critique must be total critique or it is nothing ....)

Adorno's formula of senility both prolongs and departs from these well-rehearsed dilemmas. It helps formalize what is at stake in dialectical thinking and its spectral aftermath. Can dialectic grow old and die? What does it mean for dialectics to go senile given that dialectics *is* senility; dialectic is nothing but the incessant production and formalization of obsolescence. Dialectics is degradation, deterioration, decay; there can be no dialectic that is not senile and demented. Outdatedness is the principle of dialectic. Does this mean dialectic itself will never become outdated? Is this another spin of the "quite unlosable game" of the loser wins?[43]

These are the terms with which Adorno famously launches *Negative Dialectics*: philosophy lives on because the moment to have realized it has irretrievably passed.[44] *Because* and not *although*. The failure of philosophy is not the obstacle but the ticket to its survival. Metaphysics continues on through its own irreversible demise. (If this sounds like an idle exercise in sophistry, this is probably because this, i.e. sophistry, is for Adorno more or less what (academic) philosophy has been reduced to in the epoch of its own overliving.) Speaking in a broader historical framework, Adorno speaks of the bourgeoisie's failure to die properly, by which he means its failure to find a successor—its failure to universalize, to make good its promise of freedom, to expand and consummate the liberal project.[45] This can only mean the inability or refusal of the bourgeois revolution to engender its proletariat sequel—the defeat of the proletariat revolution, the persistence of capitalism beyond its own expiration date, the foreclosure of the communist future. Overliving amounts to a crisis of testation. You cannot die if you do not have a successor, if your testament is not prepared (as Bouvard and

Pecuchet discovered the hard way when they tried to kill themselves but quickly realized that they hadn't done the necessary paperwork).[46] Like Hunter Gracchus, the bourgeoisie has missed the moment of its own death and is condemned to live on intestate. Philosophy and capitalism have this in common. They operate by the same calendar.

When exactly was that fateful moment? It's not entirely clear when the critical moment came and went, whether it was a one-off opportunity, and why the appointment could not have been rescheduled. Once you start counting, it's hard to keep track of all the missed moments, and maybe that's the point. Deleuze remarks that Nietzsche produced "twelve or thirteen versions of the death of God."[47] *Twelve or thirteen*: the count is oddly precise in its imprecision: Is this an estimate? Did Deleuze stop counting, did he lose count, did he run out of numbers? Or did he realize that the very exercise of enumeration—the faith in numbers—was in the service of another idol that would in turn need to be killed off?[48] Elsewhere, Deleuze says that there "are at least *fifteen* versions of the death of God, all of them very beautiful."[49] In yet another place, he suggests that Nietzsche was not even that interested in the death of God, that story having been played out by Feuerbach, but he expresses appreciation for the comic energy and inventiveness of Nietzsche's recapitulations. "As old stories tend to multiply their variants, Nietzsche multiplies the versions of the death of God, all of them comic or humorous."[50]

Comedy is not the mood we usually associate with Adorno, but there is something darkly funny, I dare to say absurdist, in the ever-swelling catalogue of missed moments. When exactly was that fateful hour when everything went from terrible to *really* terrible? There are many dates jostling for attention: was it 1793, the year that "Absolute Freedom" tipped into Terror; was it 1848, the year the European bourgeoisie broke ranks with the workers and careened back into counter-revolutionary mode; was it 1871, the year the Paris Commune was crushed; was it 1919, the year the German revolution was defeated; was it 1921, the defeat of the workers' council movement in Italy and the end of the Biennio Rosso; was it 1924, or 1934, or whatever date you want to assign to the collapse of the glory days of the Russian Revolution and the onset of the Stalin era? Or was it Auschwitz, when all these defeats condensed, when temporal markers ceased to provide the measure, when dates yielded to place-names, when time became space. "After Auschwitz," the preposition "after" loses all temporal meaning. For Adorno, Auschwitz retroactively transforms everything that happened before Auschwitz into the prelude to Auschwitz: the aftershock imposes a retroactive necessity on history such that everything that came before the event is drawn into the penumbra of its aftermath.[51] After Auschwitz, there will have been no before or after Auschwitz because chronology collapses. This is maybe why Adorno feels entitled to speak so blithely (and unhistorically) about human history as a single undifferentiated disaster crashing forward in a single uninterrupted swoop "from the slingshot to the atom bomb."[52] The ease with which "Auschwitz" itself turns into a timeless metonymy for atrocity-in-general—how effortlessly it will come to be sacralized, sentimentalized, instrumentalized, assigned a rank and value within the calculus of comparative atrocity—all this is another effect of the abstraction exemplified by Auschwitz.

But the very framing of the question—*When? What happened? When exactly did it happen?*—is already a confession that it's too late to answer and that we wouldn't understand the answer anyway; the question itself only proves that we are caught up in the bureaucratic rationality of timetables and schedules. This is exactly Vladimir's annoying question to Pozzo. He is unnerved when Pozzo and Lucky show up inexplicably disabled in the second act and things start up all over again. Everything is the same but different, nothing is happening, for the second time, and yet everything has changed.[53] Vladimir keeps trying to pin down the decisive moment of change: When exactly did you go blind, Pozzo, when did Lucky go dumb? Did it happen all of the sudden? Was it yesterday? No later than yesterday? When?!

Didi's obsessive concern with timing resonates with the zany preoccupation, shared by all Beckett's characters, with number-crunching and metrics, but it touches also on a fundamental anxiety about theater. What exactly *does* happen between Act One and Act Two? What happens when the lights go on, where does everybody go during intermission, where do they live between performances, what are they doing in the limbo of their offstage nonexistence? What is going on when I'm not around to witness it? We are inching back toward the primal scene.

Pozzo eventually explodes:[54]

POZZO: [*Suddenly furious.*] Have you not done tormenting me with your accursed time! It's abominable! When! When! One day, is that not enough for you, one day like any other day, one day he went dumb, one day I went blind, one day we'll go deaf, one day we were born, one day we shall die, the same day, the same second, is that not enough for you? [*Calmer.*] They give birth astride of a grave, the light gleams an instant, then it's night once more. [*He jerks the rope.*] On![55]

One can well understand Pozzo's irritation, but one can also understand the desire behind Vladimir's persistent questioning. His curiosity resonates with the insistent question voiced by both speakers in *Footfalls,* as May paces back and forth across the stage to her incessant nine-beat rhythm while her mother mutters offstage.[56] What happened, when did it happen, will you ever have done "revolving it all," her mother asks ("it?" interrupts May bewilderedly)—as if there were a discrete *it* to be recaptured, as if the moment missed were not a retroactive effect of the missing. We are looping back to the traumatic temporality of the primal scene: the insatiable fantasy, produced by coming too late, that this lateness could be assigned an hour—the longing for a single discrete moment that could be identified, date-stamped, and discharged—as if trauma itself had not destroyed the possibility of being circumscribed within the punctual enclosure of the lived moment. It is trauma that stimulates the desire for punctuality and punctuation—the desire to return to ground zero, to retrieve the zero hour, to restart clock and calendar so that everything starts again from scratch. It is trauma that produces the need for there to have been a "trauma." The drive to "revolve it all" is the impossible desire to *have it all*, or more precisely, to have *it be all*—to find an *it* capable of revealing and explaining *all*—to identify a simple big-bang moment powerful enough to produce a unified totality from the "tangle of tatters."[57] The drive for resolution is the search for a narrative lodestone powerful enough to capture the scatter such that the abyss between *it* and *all* collapses. It is ultimately the drive to escape the drivenness of the drive—to put an end to that ceaseless rotary motion, to transform this revolving into a resolving or resolution (in both senses).

But isn't this the fundamental desire of all theater? Is theater anything but the attempt to "revolve it all"—to punctuate time, to stamp a "time signature" —to stage its own withdrawal from ordinary time by imposing a minimal rhythmic structure on the amorphous temporality of everyday experience? This means, minimally, introducing a formal sequence of beginning–middle–end if only so that the play can bring itself to an end: it must make its ending a *dramatic* ending. Like the organism in *Beyond the Pleasure Principle* (we are observing the death drive in action) the play wants to "die in its own way." Every play is a waiting game, a protracted cadence in which time stretches toward an ending that is both expected and yet unbearably deferred.[58] Every play struggles against the sludge of a time in which "something seems to have occurred, something has seemed to occur, and nothing has occurred, nothing at all."[59] The play must go on, everything must repeat, everything has repeated, the play cannot end because it was over before it had even begun. "The end is in the beginning and yet you go on."[60] Beckett is formalizing the impossible drive—the drivenness—of all theater.

Is this not the perfect deflationary staging of the "senile, demented dialectic"? You know that it all ends, you even know how it will end, you know the punchline, you know that the absolute is already (yawn) with us, that the story is already ended, and yet you go on. You know it, and yet you've forgotten it and so on you go.

## Coda: "All is a—(*he yawns*)–bsolute"[61]

Generations of Hegel-bashers have gravitated to the color gray as the quintessentially anti-dialectical, non-dialectical, undialectical a-dialectical non-color. Apparently devoid of extremity, lacking any opposite, occupying no place on the color wheel, impervious to the vicissitudes of contradiction and refutation, gray would seem to put a spanner in the dialectical machinery—a term of nuance, diminishment, and indistinction that might dodge and dislodge the noxious negativities, polarities, dichotomies, binaries that seem destined to pair off for combat, reversal, and eventual reconciliation.[62]

Beckett is often enlisted in the service of these anti-dialectical shenanigans. Is there anything less binary than his dull, bleached-out palette, the haziness of his interiors and exteriors, the gray hair, gray walls, gray robes, gray rectangles on gray walls, the gray skies, the stony gray landscapes, the impossible demands on his actors for more "colorless" delivery. Even the *word* "gray" is endlessly repeated, as if gray can never be gray enough, as if there can never be enough of it.

> Scattered ruins same grey as the sand ash grey true refuge. Four square all light sheer white blank planes all gone from mind. Never was but grey air timeless no sound figment the passing light. No sound no stir ash grey sky mirrored earth mirrored sky. Never but this changelessness dream the passing hour.[63]

This is funny, because gray was Hegel's favorite color too, but no one ever praised *him* for that. In the infamous preface to his most reviled work, Hegel chooses gray as the basic color of philosophical retrospection:

> When philosophy paints its grey in grey, a shape of life has grown old, and it cannot be rejuvenated, but only recognized, by the grey in grey of philosophy; the owl of Minerva begins its flight only with the onset of dusk.[64]

But this is no ordinary gray. Hegel is talking about *very* gray, very-very-gray, grayer-than-gray, gray-*on*-gray, gray-*in*-gray—gray redoubled, and even doubly redoubled, for the repetition is immediately repeated. Hegel somehow manages to out-Beckett Beckett. In *Lessness / Sans*, Beckett's most grizzled, most gray-larded text, and formally one of his most experimental, the word "gray" appears fifty-two times over five short pages; on two separate occasions in the same text, the word is repeated four times within the space of a paragraph. In the despised preface to the *Philosophy of Right,* the word appears four times within a single sentence.

Gray: not the white light of Cartesian reason, not the blinding epiphany of the Platonic sunshine, not the lucidities of the Enlightenment, not the negative clarity of the mystical night.

Starting already in Hegel's lifetime, these words have always been taken to be the formula of Hegel's own "political conservativism, quietism, and optimism" (in the words of Rudolf Haym, one of his earliest detractors)—a confession of philosophy's capitulation to the existing order. In fairness to Hegel, all he was doing was refusing the devil's pact that had gotten Faust into so much trouble. Mephistopheles had tempted the scholar to leave his study—to leave the gray world of theory and seize the (seductively alliterative) golden-green tree of life in all its vibrancy. Hegel declined the invitation, figuring that there must be a catch, given that life was already gray anyway. You don't even have to leave the house to see this for yourself; just look out the window or get your servant to do it before he tries to leave you.

It is not simply that philosophy is old and sluggish, that it comes too late to make a difference, that it lags behind events. The more troubling point is that reality itself is laggardly: "a shape of life has grown old and cannot be rejuvenated." Gray-*on*-gray: the repetition marks the convergence or collision of two anachronisms: decrepit philosophy encounters a decrepit reality, lateness scraping against lateness, shadow upon shadow. Repetition produces the paradoxical synchronicity between two non-synchronicities. It is the key to Hegel's speculative grammar and accounts for the pulsating copula between the rational and the actual. Repetition marks the speculative identity between thought and being.

Hegel was not acquiescing to the existent. Despite the meticulous detail with which he outlines the rudiments of the rational state, he is neither endorsing any existing state nor offering a program for a future one. Hegel is not writing recipes for the cookbooks of the future. It's striking that few of the liberal institutions he describes in *Philosophy of Right* have seen the light of day in Prussia around 1820: not the jury system, not the bicameral system, not the equality of citizens before the law, not the publicity of judicature, not the freedom of the press, not even a measly constitution … Even before these modern institutions have made their appearance, Hegel is describing them as defunct beyond resuscitation.[65] Modernity is superannuated before it has come into existence.[66]

But even setting aside the weather, gray-on-gray is a peculiar color for philosophy, not least in that it undermines every image of enlightenment. It reveals the strange depths of Hegel's inverted Platonism. Plato had a point when he described the world of appearances as a world of shadows; his error was to imagine that you might escape the cave, that there was a truth awaiting you in a land of eternal sunshine. In the *Aesthetics*, Hegel describes the realm of images similarly: "only a shadow-world … no more than a surface … mere schemata."[67] But unlike Plato, Hegel means this as a compliment. In relinquishing the consoling fantasy of Nature—the "golden green" of Life in all its immediacy—art inches toward the "shadow realm of the Idea."[68] The passage from art to philosophy, from intuition to concept, is not an ascent from the shadows into the sunlight, but rather a sideways step from shadow to shadow, from the shadow to the shadow of the shadow, from one cave to another, from one theater to another. It is in this sense that Hegel describes the Olympian heights of the *Logic* as the "realm of shadows."[69]

But the figure of gray-on-gray is strange for yet another reason: it comes close to the "monochromatic formalism"—identity philosophy of all stripes—that Hegel will never stop reviling. The phrase cannot fail to evoke the gloom-on-gloom of the "night in which all cows are black." Those were the words with which Hegel had famously mocked his erstwhile comrade Schelling in 1806, understandably ruining that friendship forever.[70] In making this dig, in the Preface to the *Phenomenology,* Hegel was putting his own spin on the witticism circulating at that time among the Jena romantics. The original joke described a gray night in which all cats are gray: the quip goes back at least to *Don Quixote*; Sancho Panza gave it a misogynist spin. Who knows why Hegel decided to adjust the joke, why he changed gray cats into black cows; I doubt it was out of either feminism or chivalry. Maybe he had a sixth sense that the gray might one day come in handy, that he should steal it away from the romantics and save it for a later date; I'm not sure about the cows.

Finally: the figure is especially odd for us today, if only because of the avant-garde resonances it has ineluctably acquired since the time of Hegel's writing. Having pronounced the end of art (the end of everything), Hegel manages to describe paintings and media he could not have seen or even imagined. Having passed from the shadow land of art to the shadow realm of philosophy, Hegel has already started working his way through the history of modern painting: the monochromes of Malevich and Reinhardt; the overpainted canvases of Ryman; the blurred paintings of Richter; the grayed out alphabets of Jasper Johns; the grayness of cinema and photography; the grayness of newspapers and television screens; the gray world of administration; the gray world of capitalism—a world in which, as Marx quipped, "all theory is gray and green is the colour of business alone."[71]

# Notes

I am very grateful to Paul Kottman, David Lloyd and Jean-Michel Rabaté for their comments on an earlier version of this essay, and to Matthew Feldman for his advice about the Beckett Archive at Trinity College Dublin and for sharing his extensive knowledge of the manuscripts..

1. Samuel Beckett, "An Interview with Beckett," interview by Israel Shenker, in *Samuel Beckett, the Critical Heritage*, ed. Lawrence Graver and Raymond Federman (London/New York: Routledge and Kegan Paul, 1979), 148. The comparison is probably ill-advised for reasons I'll come to.

2. Cf. Slavoj Žižek, *The Parallax View* (Cambridge, MA/London: MIT Press, 1996), 77; cf. also Slavoj Žižek, *Absolute Recoil: Towards a New Foundation of Dialectical Materialism* (London/New York: Verso, 2014), 344–9. Mladen Dolar has trenchantly argued against the applicability of this scenario to Beckett's *Worstward Ho* in "The Endgame of Aesthetics: From Hegel to Beckett," *Problemi International* 3, no. 3 (2019): 185–214.

3. Stanley E. Gontarski, "Greying the Canon: Beckett in Performance, Beckett as Performance," in *Beckett after Beckett*, ed. Stanley E. Gontarski and Anthony Uhlmann (Gainesville: University Press of Florida, 2006), 141–57. For an account of Beckett's complex relationship to his own archive—what he himself at one point refers to as his "MS fumbling and bumbling"—see Mark Nixon, "Beckett's Manuscripts in the Marketplace," *Modernism/Modernity* 18, no. 4 (2012): 823–31.

4. Samuel Beckett in its last words of the addendum to *Watt*, ed. Chris J. Ackerley (London: Faber and Faber, 2009), 223.

5   Samuel Beckett in a telegraph to Jessica Tandy, regarding the breakneck delivery speed of *Not I*, quoted in *The Grove Companion to Samuel Beckett*, ed. Chris J. Ackerley and Stanley E. Gontarski (New York: Grove Press, 2004), 411.

6   As Samuel Beckett declares in a letter to director Alan Schneider on December 29, 1957, in *The Letters of Samuel Beckett, Volume III: 1957–1965*, ed. George Craig, Martha Dow Fehsenfeld, Dan Gunn, and Lois More Overbeck (Cambridge: Cambridge University Press, 2014), 82.

7   Cf. Samuel Beckett, "On Endgame," in *Disjecta: Miscellaneous Writings and a Dramatic Fragment*, ed. Ruby Cohn (New York: Grove Press, 1984), 95. "Endspiel wird blosses Spiel sein. Nichts weniger. Von Rätseln und Lösungen also kein Gedanke. Es gibt für solches ernstes Zeug Universitäten, Kirchen, Cafés de Commerce usw."

8   See Beckett's pronouncement in response to an interviewer's question in 1961: "Have contemporary philosopher's had any influence on your thought?
    I never read philosophers.
    Why not?
    I never understand anything they write.
    All the same, people have wondered if the existentialists' problem of being may afford a key to your works.
    There's no key or problem. I wouldn't have had any reason to write my novels if I could have expressed their subject in philosophic terms."
    Samuel Beckett in an interview with Gabriel d'Aubarède on February 16, 1961, in *Samuel Beckett: The Critical Heritag*e, ed. Graver and Federman, 217.

9   Not to exaggerate: Beckett did read real books. Among the books in his library is a marked up copy, belonging to Jean Beaufret, of L. Debricon's anthology of René Descartes, *Choix de Textes* (Paris: Louis-Michel Éditions, 1909), although it's unclear which annotations are whose. He spent the better part of a year in the Long Room of Trinity College Dublin reading Geulincx in Latin. He read Fritz Mauthner in German. He pored over Schopenhauer in German. He even took note of Schopenhauer's own admonition that you had to put aside the filter of commentary and read Kant in the original; this may be what prompted the impoverished Beckett to order the eleven-volume edition of Kant from Munich. See Samuel Beckett, letter to Thomas McGreevy on January 5, 1938, in *The Letters of Samuel Beckett Volume I: 1929–1940*, ed. Martha Dow Fehsenfeld and Lois More Overbeck (Cambridge: Cambridge University Press, 2009), 581. See also Dirk van Hulle and Mark Nixon, *Samuel Beckett's Library* (Cambridge: Cambridge University Press, 2013), 137–43 and 150. Admittedly Beckett's annotations of Kant are mainly confined to Cassirer's introduction but still, it shows good intentions. See van Hulle and Nixon for a list of the books in Beckett's possession at the time of his death. For Beckett's style of page-

bending, see ibid., 149. For a meticulous attempt at dating and tracking the literary residues of Beckett's philosophical readings see Matthew Feldman, *Beckett's Books: A Cultural History of Samuel Beckett's "Interwar Notes"* (New York/London: Continuum, 2006) and Matthew Feldman, *Falsifying Beckett: Essays on Archives, Philosophy, and Methodology in Beckett Studies* (New York: Columbia University Press, 2015).

10  See van Hulle and Nixon, *Beckett's Library*. In a letter to his first biographer, Deirdre Bair, Beckett regrets his lack of philosophical background. "Because he had not taken a philosophy course at Trinity College, which he felt was a serious defect in his education, he set out on what he thought was a systematic schedule of readings." Deirdre Bair, *Samuel Beckett: A Biography* (New York/London: Harcourt Brace Jovanovich, 1978), 91 and 695n5.

11  TCD MS 10967.

12  Wilhelm Windelband, *Geschichte der Philosophie* (Freiburg: Mohr, 1983). Beckett's notes on ancient philosophy were supplemented by a number of other sources, primarily John Burnet, *Greek Philosophy: Thales to Plato* (London: Macmillan, 1914) and Archibald Alexander, *A Short History of Philosophy* (Glasgow: Maclehose, 1908). See van Hulle and Nixon, *Beckett's Library*; see also Feldman, *Beckett's Books* and Everett C. Frost, "Catalogue of 'Notes Diverse Holo[graph],'" *Samuel Beckett Today/Aujourd'hui* 16 (2006): 19–182.

13  The collection was donated by Beckett's bequest to Trinity College Dublin and Reading University in 1997. For a description and extensive catalogue, see Frost, "Catalogue of 'Notes Diverse Holo[graph],'" as well as Feldman's invaluable *Beckett's Books*. A critical edition of the "Philosophy Notes," edited by Matthew Feldman and Steve Matthews, is forthcoming through Oxford University Press. I'm very grateful to Matthew Feldman for his generous help and to the staff at the Manuscript Collection at TCD during the summer of 2019.

14  Beckett's transition from the life of an academic to the "rest of [his] life writing books that no one will read" was far from smooth or unambivalent. As late as 1936 he was still contemplating an array of alternative careers, including commercial pilot, filmmaker (famously sending an unanswered letter to Eisenstein requesting to apprentice with him at the State Institute of Cinematography in Moscow), advertising copywriter, art critic, gallery assistant, translator… See James Knowlson, *Damned to Fame: The Life of Samuel Beckett* (London: Bloomsbury, 1996), 212. See also Beckett's letters to Thomas McGreevy from 1935 and 1936 in Beckett, *The Letters of Samuel Beckett Volume I: 1929–1940*, 171 and 362.

15  TCD MS 10967/230. On Beckett's irritated eruptions throughout the Kant notes, see Jean-Michel Rabaté, *Think Pig! Beckett at the Limits of the Human*

(New York: Fordham University Press, 2016), 99f, and passim for an elegant speculation on Beckett's philosophical resonances.

16  TCD MS 10967/252.

17  In "Gnome," a poem of 1934, Beckett writes: "Spend the years of learning squandering / Courage for the years of wandering / Through a world politely turning / From the loutishness of learning." Samuel Beckett, *Collected Poems in English and French* (London: Calder, 1977), 7. See Steven Connor, *Beckett and the Material Imagination* (Cambridge: Cambridge University Press, 2014), 152–75.

18  Samuel Beckett in a letter to Thomas McGreevy on May 26, 1938, in *The Letters of Samuel Beckett Volume I: 1929-1940*, 626.

19  http://www.fountainpennetwork.com/forum/topic/268290-samuel-beckett-manuscript/, accessed August 29, 2019.

20  Auguste Blanqui, *L'Éternité par les astres*, as quoted by Walter Benjamin, "Paris: Capital of the Nineteenth Century," in *The Arcades Project*, trans. Howard Eiland and Kevin McLaughlin (Cambridge: Harvard/Belknap, 1999), 26. Walter Benjamin copied out Blanqui's "astronomical hypothesis" repeatedly during his Paris exile.

21  "Die Grundkonzeption des Mythos ist die Welt als Strafe—die Strafe, die sich den Straffälligen erst erzeugt. Die ewige Wiederkehr ist die ins Kosmische projizierte Strafe des Nachsitzens: die Menschheit hat ihren Text in unzähligen Wiederholungen nachzuschreiben." Walter Benjamin, notes to "Über den Begriff der Geschichte," in *Gesammelte Schriften*, vol. I.3, ed. Rolf Tiedemann and Hermann Schweppenhäuser (Frankfurt am Main: Suhrkamp, 1991), 1234.

22  Walter Benjamin in a letter to Gershom Scholem on January 20, 1930, in *The Correspondence of Walter Benjamin, 1910-1930*, ed. Theodor W. Adorno and Gershom Scholem (Chicago, IL: University of Chicago Press, 1994), 359.

23  Cf. David Lloyd, *Irish Culture and Colonial Modernity 1800-2000: The Transformation of Oral Space* (Cambridge: Cambridge University Press, 2011), 198–220.

24  Samuel Beckett, "Endgame," in *The Complete Dramatic Works* (London: Faber and Faber, 1990), 94.

25  Georg Wilhelm Friedrich Hegel, *Phenomenology of Spirit*, trans. Arnold Vincent Miller (Oxford: Oxford University Press, 1977), 137f.

26  TCD MS 10967, 250r.

27  Kojève's Monday lectures on Hegel's *Phenomenology* were delivered under the title of "La Philosophie Religieuse de Hegel" at the Ecole Pratique des Hautes Études between 1933 and 1939, and attended by Georges Bataille, André Breton, Jacques Lacan, Michel Leiris, Maurice Merleau-Ponty, among others. They were edited and published by Raymond Queneau after the war as *Introduction à la lecture de Hegel* (Paris: Gallimard, 1947).

28  "Neither with you nor without you"—Beckett's description, one of the rare hints he chose to offer about his own plays, of the Hamm/Clov entwinement; the phrase is drawn from Ovid's *Amores*. See Beckett's letter to Alan Schneider on December 29, 1957, in *The Letters of Samuel Beckett, Volume III: 1957–1965*, 82.

29  Beckett, "Endgame," 97.

30  Cf. Jacques Lacan, *The Seminar, Book XXI, Les non-dupes errent, 1973–1974* (Paris: Éditions de l'association lacanienne internationale, 2010).

31  Beckett, "Endgame," 121.

32  Why? Simply because its outcome is so dire. Far from being an allegory of emancipation, the episode could be rightly understood as an account of counterrevolutionary disempowerment: Why does the slave *not* seize the freedom that is rightfully his? This question will haunt the remainder of the *Phenomenology*. Within the framework of this Master-Slave encounter, there is no prospect of liberation, no hint of revolutionary upheaval, no suggestion that the roles might reverse or transform: the slave's freedom is "notional" only (i.e. it is visible only "for us," the readers, who have assumed the position of the subject-supposed-to-know). Both Slave and Master are equally deluded about what is transpiring in their relationship and lack both the will and the resources to transform it. The most that can be salvaged by either party is the questionable dignity of Stoicism—the consoling phantasm of an abstract freedom of thought where the material distinction between oppressed and oppressor is occluded. The idea of revolution will not be properly conceptualized until the reader has slogged through several hundred pages of densely argued exposition. This deferral may be in part a symptom of Hegel's own political cautiousness, but it does introduce the idea of a revolutionary desire that is not forged on the crucible of heroic sacrifice. This puts pressure on the humanist (and at this date almost exclusively liberal) interpretations of Hegel that continue to privilege *recognition* as the core value of Hegel's ethical and political project.

33  See Rebecca Comay and Frank Ruda, *The Dash—The Other Side of Absolute Knowing* (Cambridge, MA/London: MIT Press, 2018). Adorno, thinking about Wagner, sums it up in musical terms: "The absolute is possible only as a reprise." Theodor W. Adorno, "Wagner's Relevance for Today," trans. Susan Gillespie, *Grand Street* 44 (1993): 55. Thanks to Alberto Toscano for reminding me of this passage.

34 Beckett describes Murphy's room as "windowless, like a monad. Samuel Beckett, *Murphy*, ed. James C. C. Mays (London: Faber and Faber, 2009), 114.

35 It also makes for peculiar novels. And, as the following examples suggest, it furthermore troubles the clear dichotomy between plays and novels, between Beckett's dramatic and his prose texts, and between the spoken and the written word more generally, complicating his avowed wish "to keep our genres distinct."

36 See Daniel Albright's illuminating discussion in *Beckett and Aesthetics* (Cambridge: Cambridge University Press, 2003), see also Beckett's 1956 letter to Alan Schneider about the staging of *Godot*, and his rejection of theater in the round, in *The Letters of Samuel Beckett, Volume II: 1941–1956*, ed. George Craig, Martha Dow Fehsenfeld, Dan Gunn, and Lois More Overbeck (Cambridge: Cambridge University Press, 2011), 593–6. It is notable that when it comes to painting, however, Beckett praises Bram van Velde for pushing beyond the convention of Renaissance perspective where "everything is within the realm of the *possible*." Samuel Beckett, "Three Dialogues" with Georges Duthuit, in *Disjecta*, 139. For a penetrating discussion of painting and theater in Beckett see David Lloyd, *Beckett's Thing: Painting and Theatre* (Edinburgh: Edinburgh University Press, 2016).

37 Samuel Beckett in a letter to Alan Schneider on October 15, 1956, in *The Letters of Samuel Beckett, Volume II*, 659.

38 Theodor W. Adorno, *Aesthetic Theory*, trans. Robert Hullot-Kentor (Minneapolis: University of Minnesota Press, 1997), 251.

39 For traces of the Irish famine in Beckett's writings, see James McNaughton, *Samuel Beckett and the Politics of Aftermath* (Oxford: Oxford University Press, 2018), 137–63; David Lloyd, "Frames of Referrance: Samuel Beckett as an Irish Question," in *Beckett and Ireland*, ed. Seán Kennedy (Cambridge: Cambridge University Press, 2010), 31–55; and Julianne Ulin, "'Buried! Who Would Have Buried Her?' Famine 'Ghost Graves' in Samuel Beckett's *Endgame*," in *Hungry Words: Images of Famine in the Irish Canon*, ed. George Cusack and Sarah Goss (Dublin: Irish Academic Press, 2016), 197–222. McNaughton draws attention to the simultaneity of different famine allusions in Beckett (the Irish famine, the starvation politics of Hitler and Stalin).

40 Theodor W. Adorno, "Trying to Understand Endgame," in *Notes to Literature*, vol. I, ed. Rolf Tiedemann, trans. Shierry Weber Nicholsen (New York: Columbia University Press, 1991), 259.

41 Samuel Beckett, "Footfalls," in *The Complete Dramatic Works* (London: Faber and Faber, 1990), 400.

42  Friedrich Nietzsche, *Ecce Homo: How to Become What You Are*, trans. Duncan Large (Oxford: Oxford University Press, 2007), 88.

43  Philip Larkin, "Annus Mirabilis," in *Collected Poems*, ed. Anthony Thwaite (London: Faber & Faber, 2014).

44  Theodor W. Adorno, *Negative Dialectics*, trans. Ernest B. Ashton (London: Bloomsbury, 1981), 3.

45  Theodor W. Adorno, "Notes on Kafka," in *Prisms*, trans. Samuel Weber and Shierry Weber (Cambridge, MA/London: MIT Press, 1983), 260.

46  I explore this in Rebecca Comay, "Testament of the Revolution," *Mosaic* 50 (2017): 1–12.

47  Gilles Deleuze and Felix Guattari, *Anti-Oedipus: Capitalism and Schizophrenia*, with a preface by Michel Foucault, trans. Robert Hurley, Mark Seem, and Helen R. Lane (Minneapolis: University of Minnesota Press, 1983), 106.

48  Nietzsche is adept in showing God's talent for resurrecting—the pieties of morality, the scrupulosities of science, the abstractions of philosophy, the delusions of art, the faith in grammar, the disciplined intensities of hedonism, the zealotry of atheism itself. Is the desire for arithmetic precision, for a final tally, another avatar of the ascetic ideal? Is Deleuze's (playful) compulsion to *count* the ways of dying an expression of the desire to drive a final nail in the coffin—to declare God dead once and for all?

49  Gilles Deleuze, *Pure Immanence: Essays on a Life*, trans. Anne Boyman (New York: Zone Books, 2001), 72.

50  Gilles Deleuze, *Foucault*, trans. Seán Hand (Minneapolis: University of Minnesota Press, 1988), 129.

51  Cf. Eva Geulen, *The End of Art: Readings in a Rumour after Hegel* (Stanford, CA: Stanford University Press, 2006), 96.

52  Adorno, *Negative Dialectics*, 320. Cf. Theodor W. Adorno, *History and Freedom: Lectures 1964–1965* (Cambridge: Polity Press, 2006), 14.

53  Cf. Vivian Mercier, "The Uneventful Event," *Irish Times*, February 18, 1956.

54  VLADIMIR: I'm asking you if it came on you all of a sudden.
    POZZO: I woke up one fine day as blind as Fortune. [*Pause.*] Sometimes I wonder if I'm not still asleep.
    VLADIMIR: And when was that?
    POZZO: I don't know.
    VLADIMIR: But no later than yesterday –
    POZZO: [*Violently.*] Don't question me! The blind have no notion of time. The things of time are hidden from them too …
    Samuel Beckett, "Waiting for Godot," *The Complete Dramatic Works* (London: Faber and Faber, 1990), 80.

And a little later, à propos of Lucky:
VLADIMIR: Dumb! Since when?
Ibid., 83.

55  Ibid.

56  See David Lloyd's excellent discussion in "Frames of Referrance: Samuel Beckett as an Irish Question," in *Beckett and Ireland*, ed. Seán Hand (Cambridge: Cambridge University Press, 2010), 44–5.

57  Beckett, "Footfalls," 402. (The phrase "It all," one of the alternative titles that Beckett had considered, will be the very last words of the play, repeated three times, as the lights "fade out," and then "fade up" yet again, "even a little less still.") Ibid., 403.

58  Beckett foregrounded this dilation in his 20-second long dramaticule *Breath*, which consists entirely of the interval between opening and closing.

59  Samuel Beckett, "Happy Days," in *The Complete Dramatic Works* (London: Faber and Faber, 1990), 154.

60  Beckett, "Endgame"(riffing on T.S. Eliot), 126.

61  Ibid., 93.

62  For a more extended discussion, see my "GRREY!" essay, forthcoming in Aron Vinegar and Kamini Vellodi, eds., *Grey on Grey*: On the Threshold of Philosophy and Art (Edinburgh: Edinburgh University Press, 2021).

63  Samuel Beckett, "Lessness," in *Complete Short Prose, 1929–1989*, edited and with an Introduction and Notes by Stanley E. Gontarski (New York: Grove Press, 1992), 197. I'm indebted to Laura Salisbury for her very astute presentation at the "Grey on Grey" conference in Oslo, May 2018, essay forthcoming in Aron Vinegar and Kamini Vellodi, eds., *Grey on Grey*. On the Threshold of Philosophy and Art (Edinburgh University Press).

64  Georg Wilhelm Friedrich Hegel, *Elements of the Philosophy of Right*, trans. Hugh Barr Nisbet (Cambridge: Cambridge University Press, 1991), 23.

65  See Rebecca Comay, *Mourning Sickness: Hegel and the French Revolution* (Stanford, CA: Stanford University Press, 2011).

66  The sentiment clashes with the celebratory mood of Hegel's exhortation to enjoy just two short paragraphs earlier—"Hic Rhodus, hic salta." *Here is the rose, dance here*. Hegel had been gazing at the world through rose-tinted glasses: the present was now, the flowers were blooming, and things ran on time. The transition from the first passage to the second, from the rose to the owl, is as startling as the shift that takes place during the brief interval between *Quad I* to *Quad II*, when the color is suddenly extinguished, the sound is muted, and the movement on stage dramatically slows down. (Beckett describes the interval between the two acts as "100,000 years long.")

67  Georg Wilhelm Friedrich Hegel, *Aesthetics: Lectures on Fine Art*, vol. I, trans. Thomas Malcolm Knox (Oxford: Oxford University Press, 1975), 39.

68  Hegel, *Aesthetics*, vol. I, 5.

69  Georg Wilhelm Friedrich Hegel, *Science of Logic*, trans. George di Giovanni (Cambridge: Cambridge University Press, 2010), 37.

70  Hegel, *Phenomenology of Spirit*, 9.

71  Marx in a letter to Engels on July 20, 1862. Marx continues sardonically: "Unfortunately, I have come to realise this too late." Karl Marx and Frederick Engels. *Collected Works*, vol. 41, *Letters 1860–1864* (London: Lawrence & Wishart, 2010), 411.

# Bibliography

Ackerley, Chris J., and Stanley E. Gontarski. *The Grove Companion to Samuel Beckett*. New York: Grove Press, 2004.

Adorno, Theodor W. *Negative Dialectics*, translated by E. B. Ashton. London: Bloomsbury, 1981.

Adorno, Theodor W. "Notes on Kafka." In *Prisms*, translated by Samuel and Shierry Weber, 243–71. Cambridge, MA/London: MIT Press, 1983.

Adorno, Theodor W. "Trying to Understand Endgame." In *Notes to Literature*, vol. I, edited by Rolf Tiedemann, translated by Shierry Weber Nicholsen, 241–75. New York: Columbia University Press, 1991.

Adorno, Theodor W. "Wagner's Relevance for Today," translated by Susan Gillespie. *Grand Street*, 44 (1993): 32–59.

Adorno, Theodor W. *Aesthetic Theory*, translated by Robert Hullot-Kentor. Minneapolis: University of Minnesota Press, 1997.

Adorno, Theodor W. *History and Freedom: Lectures 1964–1965*. Cambridge: Polity Press, 2006.

Albright, Daniel. *Beckett and Aesthetics*. Cambridge: Cambridge University Press, 2003.

Alexander, Archibald. *A Short History of Philosophy*. Glasgow: Maclehose, 1908.

Bair, Deirdre. *Samuel Beckett: A Biography*. New York/London: Harcourt Brace Jovanovich, 1978.

Beckett, Samuel. *Collected Poems in English and French*. London: Calder, 1977.

Beckett, Samuel. "An Interview with Becket." Interview by Israel Shenker. In *Samuel Beckett, the Critical Heritage*, edited by Lawrence Graver and Raymond Federman, 146–8. London/New York: Routledge and Kegan Paul, 1979.

Beckett, Samuel. "On Endgame." In *Disjecta: Miscellaneous Writings and a Dramatic Fragment*, edited by Ruby Cohn, 95. New York: Grove Press, 1984.

Beckett, Samuel. "Three Dialogues." In *Disjecta: Miscellaneous Writings and a Dramatic Fragment*, edited by Ruby Cohn, 117–23. New York: Grove Press, 1984.

Beckett, Samuel. "Endgame." In *The Complete Dramatic Works*, 89–134. London: Faber and Faber, 1990.

Beckett, Samuel. "Footfalls." In *The Complete Dramatic Works*, 397–403. London: Faber and Faber, 1990.

Beckett, Samuel. "Happy Days." In *The Complete Dramatic Works*, 135–68. London: Faber and Faber, 1990.

Beckett, Samuel. "Waiting for Godot." In *The Complete Dramatic Works*, 7–88. London: Faber and Faber, 1990.

Beckett, Samuel. "Lessness." In *The Complete Short Prose: 1929–1989*, edited by Stanley E. Gontarski, 197–201. New York: Grove Press, 1995.

Beckett, Samuel. *The Letters of Samuel Beckett, Volume I: 1929–1940*, edited by Martha Dow Fehsenfeld and Lois More Overbeck. Cambridge: Cambridge University Press, 2009.

Beckett, Samuel. *Murphy*, edited by James C. C. Mays. London: Faber and Faber, 2009.

Beckett, Samuel. *Watt*, edited by Chris J. Ackerley. London: Faber and Faber, 2009.

Beckett, Samuel. *The Letters of Samuel Beckett, Volume II: 1941–56*, edited by George Craig, Martha Dow Fehsenfeld, Dan Gunn, and Lois More Overbeck. Cambridge: Cambridge University Press, 2011.

Beckett, Samuel. *The Letters of Samuel Beckett, Volume III: 1957–1965*, edited by George Craig, Martha Dow Fehsenfeld, Dan Gunn, and Lois More Overbeck. Cambridge: Cambridge University Press, 2014.

Benjamin, Walter. *Gesammelte Schriften*, edited by Rolf Tiedemann and Hermann Schweppenhäuser. Frankfurt am Main: Suhrkamp, 1991.

Benjamin, Walter. *The Correspondence of Walter Benjamin, 1910–1930*, edited by Theodor W. Adorno and Gershom Scholem. Chicago: University of Chicago Press, 1994.

Benjamin, Walter. "Paris: Capital of the Nineteenth Century." In *The Arcades Project*, translated by Howard Eiland and Kevin McLaughlin. Cambridge: Harvard/Belknap, 1999.

Burnet, John. *Greek Philosophy: Thales to Plato*. London: Macmillan, 1914.

Comay, Rebecca. *Mourning Sickness: Hegel and the French Revolution*. Stanford: Stanford University Press, 2011.

Comay, Rebecca. "Testament of the Revolution." *Mosaic* 50 (2017), 1–12.

Comay, Rebecca and Ruda, Frank. *The Dash—the Other Side of Absolute Knowing*. Cambridge, MA/London: MIT Press, 2018.

Connor, Steven. *Beckett and the Material Imagination*. Cambridge: Cambridge University Press, 2014.
Deleuze, Gilles. *Foucault*, translated by Seán Hand. Minneapolis: University of Minnesota Press, 1988.
Deleuze, Gilles. *Pure Immanence: Essays on a Life*, translated by Anne Boyman. New York: Zone Books, 2001.
Deleuze, Gilles and Guattari, Felix. *Anti-Oedipus: Capitalism and Schizophrenia*, with a preface by Michel Foucault, translated by Robert Hurley, Mark Seem, and Helen R. Lane. Minneapolis: University of Minnesota Press, 1983.
Descartes, René. *Choix de Textes*. Paris: Louis-Michel Éditions, 1909.
Dolar, Mladen. "The Endgame of Aesthetics: From Hegel to Beckett." *Problemi International* 3, no. 3 (2019): 185–214.
Feldman, Matthew. *Beckett's Books: A Cultural History of Samuel Beckett's "Interwar Notes."* New York/London: Continuum, 2006.
Feldman, Matthew. *Falsifying Beckett: Essays on Archives, Philosophy, and Methodology in Beckett Studies*. New York: Columbia University Press, 2015.
The Fountain Pen Network. "Samuel Beckett Manuscript," http://www.fountainpennetwork.com/forum/topic/268290-samuelbeckett-manuscript/, ccessed August 29, 2019.
Frost, Everett C. "Catalogue of 'Notes Diverse Holo'[graph]," *Samuel Beckett Today/Aujourd'hui* 16 (2006): 19–182.
Geulen, Eva. *The End of Art: Readings in a Rumour after Hegel*. Stanford: Stanford University Press, 2006.
Gontarski, Stanley E. "Greying the Canon: Beckett in Performance, Beckett as Performance." In *Beckett after Beckett*, edited by Stanley E. Gontarski and Anthony Uhlmann, 141–57. Gainesville: University Press of Florida, 2006.
Hegel, Georg Wilhelm Friedrich. *Aesthetics: Lectures on Fine Art*, vol. I, translated by T. M. Knox. Oxford: Oxford University Press, 1975.
Hegel, Georg Wilhelm Friedrich. *Phenomenology of Spirit*, translated by A. V. Miller. Oxford: Oxford University Press, 1977.
Hegel, Georg Wilhelm Friedrich. *Elements of the Philosophy of Right*, translated by H. B. Nisbet. Cambridge: Cambridge University Press, 1991.
Hegel, Georg Wilhelm Friedrich. *Science of Logic*, translated by George di Giovanni. Cambridge: Cambridge University Press, 2010.
Knowlson, James. *Damned to Fame: The Life of Samuel Beckett*. London: Bloomsbury, 1996.
Kojève, Alexandre. *Introduction à la lecture de Hegel*. Paris: Gallimard, 1947.
Lacan, Jacques. *The Seminar, Book XXI, Les non-dupes errent, 1973–1974*, Paris: Éditions de l'association lacanienne internationale, 2010.
Larkin, Philip. "Annus Mirabilis." In *Collected Poems*, edited by Anthony Thwaite, 199. London: Faber & Faber, 2003.
Lloyd, David. "Frames of Referrance: Samuel Beckett as an Irish Question." In *Beckett and Ireland*, edited by Seán Kennedy, 31–55. Cambridge: Cambridge University Press, 2010.

Lloyd, David. *Irish Culture and Colonial Modernity 1800–2000: The Transformation of Oral Space*. Cambridge: Cambridge University Press, 2011.
Lloyd, David. *Beckett's Thing: Painting and Theatre*. Edinburgh: Edinburgh University Press, 2016.
Marx, Karl and Frederick, Engels. *Collected Works*, vol. 41, *Letters 1860–1864*. London: Lawrence & Wishart, 2010.
McNaughton, James. *Samuel Beckett and the Politics of Aftermath*. Oxford: Oxford University Press, 2018.
Mercier, Vivian. "The Uneventful Event." *Irish Times*, February 18, 1956.
Nietzsche, Friedrich. *Ecce Homo: How to Become What You Are*, translated by Duncan Large. Oxford: Oxford University Press, 2007.
Nixon, Mark. "Beckett's Manuscripts in the Marketplace." *Modernism/Modernity* 18, no. 4 (2012): 823–31.
Nixon, Mark and Van Hulle, Dirk. *Samuel Beckett's Library*. Cambridge: Cambridge University Press, 2013.
Rabaté, Michel. *Think Pig! Beckett at the Limits of the Human*. New York: Fordham University Press, 2016.
Ulin, Julianne. "'Buried! Who Would Have Buried Her?' Famine 'Ghost Graves' in Samuel Beckett's *Endgame*." In *Hungry Words: Images of Famine in the Irish Canon*, edited by George Cusack and Sarah Goss, 197–222. Dublin: Irish Academic Press, 2016.
Windelband, Wilhelm. *Geschichte der Philosophie*. Freiburg: Mohr, 1983.
Žižek, Slavoj. *The Parallax View*. Cambridge, MA/London: MIT Press, 1996.
Žižek, Slavoj. *The Absolute Recoil: Towards a New Foundation of Dialectical Materialism*. London/New York: Verso, 2014.

# V

# Beckett's *Unnamable* Realism

## Eva Heubach

One of the most distinctive features of Samuel Beckett's work undoubtedly is the crowd of peculiar couple-characters wandering through and about his literary landscape: Vladimir and Estragon, Pozzo and Lucky, Hamm and Clov, Nagg and Nell, Willie and Winnie—to name but a few. As one can already gather from this cursory enumeration, the most famous representatives of this typically Beckettian species certainly originate from Beckett's successful theater plays. Of particular relevance, they are, however, to his novels. For it is in these novels—and, as will be shown, *through* these novels even *beyond* them—that the couple-characters function as a veritable structure-forming principle. They are, as will be shown, an embodiment of a particular impossibility at the center of what can be said to be Beckett's *Unnamable* Realism.

The very first Beckettian couple-character, Neary and Wylie, appears already in *Murphy* (1938/1947), Beckett's first novel, which means that the origin of Beckett's novel-work immediately coincides with the origin of his peculiar couple-characters.[1] However, Neary and Wylie are by no means the only double in this debut novel, for they are being redoubled yet again by an entire second line of further double-constellations. As Paul Shields has taken the trouble to highlight, there are "two coroners, two homosexuals, two waitresses, two fortune-tellers, two alcoholics, two Hindus, two alumni of Neary's academy, two scholars, two doctors, two men with tiny heads and two men with large heads."[2] This twinning-mechanism spills right over in Beckett's following novel, *Watt* (1953/1968), for here, too, the central couple-character of Watt and Knott is being redoubled yet again by a second line of further couple-characters: "Art and Con, Rose and Cerise, Cream and Berry, Blind Bill and Maimed Matt."[3]

Undeniably, Beckett's texts confront us with a curious compulsion to repeat, or more precisely and as Mladen Dolar has pointed out, with a curious *compulsion to redouble*.[4] Each couple-character immediately evokes another couple-character, each double immediately redoubles yet again. Within Beckett's novels, however, this process of redoubling takes on a unique form in that it does not restrict itself to the character's text of origin (as is the case in Beckett's plays), but instead, carries on even beyond the textual boundaries, right into the subsequent novels.

As with all of Beckett's "creatures," as the author liked to call his characters, it also holds for his novel-characters that, however hard they might try, they just cannot come to an end.[5] "Immortality" would, however, be the wrong expression for this state. It is not that Beckett's creatures live forever; rather, they simply can not stop dying. Yet, what distinguishes the "heroes" of Beckett's novels is that in this undead state, they don't just linger within the confines of their original text. Not only do they die across entire novels, but they keep on dying – even *beyond the textual margins*. Even after their novel has already ended and the book has already been closed, they still can't stop *going* and thus *coming to an end*, continuing their (impossible) existence beyond the textual margins, passing on and over into one of the subsequent novels.

Thus, it seems to be no coincidence that *going* (on) is the main occupation, if not the defining form of existence (or rather, insistence) of these liminal figures. Beckett's creatures go and walk, they creep and crawl, proceeding from one novel to the next, reappearing in constantly changing incarnations as shadows of—that is, in difference to—themselves. Beckett's novel characters, therefore, not only tend to take on the form of ceaseless, ever ongoing doubles, but they also don't cease to redouble, going on and on.[6]

One of the consequences of the creature's unending progression, their ongoing movement of migration and redoubling, is that they continually increase in numbers, ultimately forming a veritable herd. Another consequence is that the novels themselves, all the while being independent of one another, ultimately take on the form of a series—a series that, due to the bilingualism of Beckett's writing, finds itself (how could it be any different) redoubled yet again in its very serial form, running in the order of its chronological genesis from *Murphy* (1938) / *Murphy* (1947) to *Watt* (1953) / *Watt* (1968), *Mercier et Camier* (1970) / *Mercier and Camier* (1974), *Molloy* (1951) / *Molloy* (1955), *Malone meurt* (1951) / *Malone Dies* (1956), to finally *L'Innommable* (1953) / *The Unnamable* (1958).[7]

That this succession of novels constitutes a series in the very conceptual sense of the word is evidenced by several of Beckett's comments. For instance, when he writes about *Watt* in a letter to his friend George Reavy: "It is an unsatisfactory book, written in dribs and drabs, first on the run, then one evening after the clodhopping, during the occupation. But it has its place in the series, as will perhaps appear in time."[8] Or to his close friend Thomas MacGreevy about *Molloy*: "*Molloy* is a long book, the second last of the series begun with *Murphy*, if it can be said to be a series. The last is begun and then I hope I'll hear no more of him."[9] And again a few months later regarding *Malone meurt*: "I am now retyping, for rejection by the publishers, *Malone Meurt*, the last I hope of the series *Murphy, Watt, Mercier & Camier, Molloy*."[10] These quotes are interesting for at least two reasons. Not only do they bear witness to the fact that Beckett himself repeatedly referred to his novelistic work as a series, which makes the marking of *Molloy* / *Molloy*, *Malone meurt* / *Malone Dies*, and *L'Innommable* / *The Unnamable* as a separable structural unit in the form of a trilogy appear problematic.[11] Moreover, these quotes offer insight into the processuality of the series itself, that is, into the series' very own *going (on)* since all of them are pointing to a question necessarily linked to any form of seriality—namely, that of its eventual end. When can a series ever be said to be brought to completion and to have reached an end? In other words: When can a series—or anything, for that matter—be said to have finally formed a totality?

If Beckett hopes that *Watt*, his second novel, will ultimately find its place "in the series, as will perhaps appear in time," if he speaks of *Molloy* as "the second last of the series," and ultimately of *Malone meurt* as "the last I hope of the series," what he alludes to with all of these commentaries is a chronology and an end of the serial movement—an end that, however, due to the series' subsequent continuation in the form of *L'Innommable, will go on* receding. What is more, this very movement of going on finds itself inscribed in the bilingual double of the novels themselves. For example, in one of the numerous auto-referential passages in the French *Molloy* where one can read:

> Cette fois-ci, puis encore une je pense, puis c'en sera fini je pense, de ce monde-là aussi. C'est le sens de l'avant-dernier. […] De sorte qu'on se dit, j'arriverai bien cette fois-ci, puis encore une autre, peut-être, puis ce sera tout.[12]

And then in the English *Molloy*, where the passage is changed to reflect the serie's progress that has taken place in the interval between the translation from one side of the doubled text to the other:

> This time, then once more I think, *then perhaps a last time*, then I think it'll be over, with that world too. Premonition of the last but one *but one*. […]. So that you say, I'll manage this time, then perhaps once more, *then perhaps a last time*, then nothing more.[13]

What we can thus derive from these quotes is that the halting albeit relentless course of the creatures, their unending going to an end, not only makes for the series to become a series in the first place. Moreover, it causes the series itself to progress and go on with equally halting persistence. Not only is the series driven and propelled by the ongoing movement of its creatures, starting with Murphy, who, one day, chased out of his rocking-chair, supposes, "I have to go out?."[14] Furthermore, it takes up (and takes on) this very motion, all the way to the Unnamable, who, "one day, off it goes on […] simply stayed in […] instead of going out,"[15] and who from this very "within" does nothing else than to go on, eventually leading the series to its own paradoxical ending: "You must go on, I can't go on, I'll go on."[16]

How are we to understand this paradoxical, this *impossible* ending? How are we to make sense of this peculiar "going on" that arises amid the contradictory injunction of "can't" and "must," and that constitutes the paradoxical explicit of Beckett's *L'Innommable / The Unnamable*—and with it of his series of novels?[17]

---

Ever since his early days as a writer, Beckett had felt his writing to be associated with a sense of acute inability or incapacity, that is, with a sense of impossibility:

> "I can't start the *Proust*.";[18] "I have not put pen to paper on *Proust*. […] I am supposed to be going on with the Joyce too, […], God help & save me. I can't do the bloody thing.";[19] "You know I can't write at all. The simplest sentence is a torture";[20] "I can't

write anything at all, can't imagine even to shape a sentence";[21] "I haven't tried to write. The idea itself of writing seems somehow ludicrous."[22]

The writing of *L'Innommable*, however, had brought this sentiment to an unprecedented pitch. While Beckett acknowledged that "it was always submission with me," [23] he was sure that this particular time, he had veritably gone further than ever before: "I overdid it with *L'Innommable*, I mean beyond the joke."[24] With *L'Innommable* Beckett was persuaded of having arrived at "the end of the jaunt,"[25] convinced of having hit "the bottom of the barrel,"[26] of having reached an ultimate impasse and thus the end of his life as a writer:

"I think my writing days are over. *L'Innommable* finished me or expressed my finishedness."[27] "I feel more and more that I shall perhaps never be able to write anything else. Niemand wandelt unbestraft on the road that leads to *L'Innommable*. I can't go on and I can't get back."[28] "*L'Innommable* landed me in a situation I can't extricate myself from."[29]

Even during the subsequent translation of the novel, this feeling of impossibility—having to go on while not being able to—troubled him with the same if not with heightened intensity. He described the undertaking as "horrifyingly difficult,"[30] felt it to be a "torture—and nothing can come of it,"[31] a "losing battle,"[32]—quite simply an *impossible* task:

"Have started the *impossible* job of translating *L'Innommable* and gave it up the other day in loathing. Shall be fifty (50) in a month's time and can well believe it. 18.000 days and not much to show for them. Better stop before I start. No news anyway. Just jog along, on the flat of my back 15 hours of the 24."[33]—"I should be translating *L'Innommable*, but it's an *impossible* job."[34]—"I am supposed to be translating *L'Innommable*, which is *impossible*. Not a sound all day and night but of the carts heaped high with the last mangels. No more heights, no more depths, the doldrums."[35]

Beckett's attempts to get out of the literary cul-de-sac *L'Innommable* had left him in went on for several years. Already in 1951, he wrote to his publisher Jérôme Lindon concerning *L'Innommable*: "It is this last work that I am most attached to, although it has left me in a sorry state. I'm trying to get over it. But I am not getting over it."[36] And in the following years, he repeatedly spoke of the temptation to give up on writing altogether, indeed of the downright hope to finally be able to resign:

> "If I could make the decision to give up, it might be better."[37]—"Never felt less like writing and I haven't felt like it for years, and never so revolted at the thought of work done. Sometimes feel like letting myself be sucked in by this exquisite morass, just lie down and give up and do nothing more. Always felt that temptation here but never so strong as these last weeks."[38]—"I am in acute crisis about my work (on the lines familiar to you by now) and have decided that I not merely can't but won't go on."[39]

If Beckett did not resign from his literary work at any point, if ultimately he was never able to stop writing – just like one of his "creatures," continually "struggling to struggle on from where the

*Unnamable* left me off, that is with the next next to nothing"[40]—this should, in turn, not be read as proof that he eventually managed to escape the impasse created by *L'Innommable / The Unnamable* and thus to dispense with the impossibility. Instead, he recognized in the exploration of this impasse his very own way of "going on," directly targeting and seeking it out, choosing the systematic movement from one literary and aesthetic dead-end to the next to be his literary method: "To write is impossible but not yet impossible enough. That's how I cod myself these days."[41] The novel *L'Innommable / The Unnamable* thus not only represents a veritable dead-end and hence a point of impossibility within Beckett's writing experience, but it also prefigures a procedure that was to be formative for his remaining oeuvre. As Beckett once spontaneously noted about his literary activity: "Yes, that's it! Can't and must! That's my situation."[42] Or as the Unnamable has it: "That the impossible should be asked of me, good, what else could be asked of me?"[43]

———

Another indication that *L'Innommable / The Unnamable* indeed constitutes a paradoxical endpoint not only in Beckett's own experience as a writer but also in his series of novels can be found if we shift the focus back to the level of the novel characters and their ongoing movement of migration and redoubling. For, it is in this last novel of the series that all the characters, "at least from Murphy on," come together for a final reunion: The whole "troop of lunatics," "all these Murphys, Molloys and Malones," are gathering around the "big talking ball" that is the Unnamable, "wheeling about" him "like a planet about its sun."[44] Not only does this final parade offer the chance to cast a last glance at all the creatures, the whole "ponderous chronicle of moribunds in their courses, moving, clashing, writhing or fallen in short-lived swoons."[45] Moreover, it is on the occasion of this final convention, as the creatures are gathering to ring in the series' impossible ending, that Beckett introduces, as if en passant, a telling designation for the notorious couple-characters that set the series in motion in the first place—a designation that may well provide an entry-point into an exploration of this specific impossibility that seems to be at the heart of Beckett's (novelistic) project: "Two shapes then, oblong like man, entered into collision before me. They fell and I saw them no more. I naturally thought of the pseudocouple Mercier-Camier."[46] What does Beckett allude to when he designates his couple-characters as "pseudocouples" rather than merely as "couples"? Why "pseudo-"?

As with any binary arrangement, it indeed is tempting to think of Beckett's doubles as of two entities that, although they are in clear opposition to one another, ultimately represent but two complementary parts of one single whole—a logic that can be said to abide by the pattern "If 'Watt' is the question than 'Knott' is the answer,"[47] and that has been applied and adopted by many of Beckett's critics in precisely this manner. However, Beckett himself gives us a hint that points in another direction when he explains the logic of the pseudocouple as that of *"nec tecum nec sine te."*[48] "Not with you, nor without you," the pseudocouple is defined by the very fact that it consists of two entities that by no means are complementary and amount to a homogeneous whole—but rather of two entities that *cannot* be together, *nor* be apart. The two sides of the pseudocouple *cannot* be together, say, in (a) relation to one another. But since at the same time—and paradoxically so—they *cannot not* be together, they are also *not not* in a relation to one another. Instead, they portray *a third option* arising from this very impasse, namely, the option of an active *non-relation*. To put it yet differently: With the pseudocouple we are not dealing with *two of one* kind (*Zwei* von *Einem*), nor with a *Oneness* formed out of *two* (die *Einheit* einer *Zwei*), but with a paradoxical union, *united in their very discord* and tied together by an invisible "bond of division."[49]

In this sense, the pseudocouple can be said to be the very epitome of the paradoxical impasse of "can't" and "must"—a *logical* structure that, rendered in *chronological* terms, embodies the paradoxical temporality of being always already over (since they were never and will never be able to form a union) and still going on unendingly (since they cannot separate either) that must be the specific chronos of the *ongoing going on* of the novel's ending.

---

However, Beckett's novels have not only engendered a multitude of these odd pairs within their literary universe. They have also generated (at least) one of them outside the textual margins—namely, the pseudocouple of Georg Lukács and Theodor W. Adorno. With them, one is confronted with two competing dialectical systems—that is, with two competing conceptualizations of totality, deriving from two competing readings of Hegel.[50] Although their respective conceptions of totality, and thus their understanding of what dialectic is and should be, clearly contradict one another—in fact, are diametrically opposed to each other—the work of the two thinkers is nonetheless intertwined in the most peculiar and most intimate ways.[51] Their relationship spans all stages of their philosophical lives, ranging from profound admiration to sheer disgust, ultimately finding its point of culmination in the notorious twentieth-century debate about realist aesthetics.[52]

If one takes a closer look at the points of intersection of their work, where both of them deliberately refer to each other, or where they clash and end up in one of their fierce controversies, one cannot but notice that right at these points of "intersection" there is always one specific name to be found, one name that stands out in particular: Not only is the name "Beckett" being mentioned with particular frequency, but it is in connection to this name that one can read the most violently divergent commentaries, it is this name that engenders the harshest fights, and it is this name that appears to encourage both of the opponents to formulate their position in the most drastic manner, insulting each other in the most abrasive (and oftentimes most comic) ways possible.

One notorious example is Adorno's "Extorted Reconciliation," a text about which Adorno writes that it should be read in systematic connection with his essay on Beckett's *Endgame*,[53] and in which he famously states that "it was probably in *The Destruction of Reason* that the destruction of Lukács' own reason manifested itself most crassly,"[54] accusing Lukács of "the stultification that befalls even the most intelligent when they fall in line with directives like those ordaining socialist realism."[55] Lukács, on the other hand, counters these insults with an equally famous reply, reproaching Adorno of having taken up "residence in the 'Grand Hotel Abyss'" which he describes as "a beautiful hotel, equipped with every comfort, on the edge of an abyss of nothingness, of absurdity. And the daily contemplation of the abyss between excellent meals or artistic entertainment, can only heighten the enjoyment of the subtle comforts offered."[56] Adorno, in turn, takes up this image to again turn it against his adversary: "Lukács has thrown himself into the abyss and misjudged this as salvation; he is not even here but is crawling around down there, broken like one of the Beckett-figures about whom he is so indignant."[57] Considering the vehement reactions during this debate, one is inclined to ask: What is really at stake in this controversy? And, more importantly, what role does Beckett play in it?

———

For Georg Lukács, the task of realist literature consists in the depiction of society as a whole, of society in its totality—a task that he takes to be grounded in Hegel's notorious dictum "The True is the whole."[58] While Lukács does not believe this dictum to be *already* true, that is, to *already* having found its realization in the world as it is, what he gathers from it is the imperative to make it *become* true—as he famously states in *History and Class Consciousness*: "What is crucial is that there should be an *aspiration towards* totality."[59] Moreover, it is precisely the realist novel—and not philosophy—to which he attributes the historical mission to envision a *narrative translation of this imperative into reality*.

Against the backdrop of this conception of realism, Lukács detects two currents of what he calls "modernist anti-realism": Naturalism on the one hand and Formalism on the other.[60] While Naturalism's "wrong objectivism" renders a picture of human beings as passive victims of cataclysmic forces beyond their control, Formalism's "wrong subjectivism" pictures individual subjects as monadic beings, circling within their opaque, impenetrable incognito around what they experience as their existential despair. However, as they take this despair to be the general "*condition humaine,*" they fail to recognize it as simply the historical condition of capitalism.[61] Thus, both of these tendencies end up merely adopting "the ideological complement of their historical position" and consequently misrepresent the nature of totality, as they fail to adapt "the Hegelian view that the inner and outer world form an objective dialectical unity, that they are indissolubly married in spite their apparent opposition."[62]

The literary current under which Lukács subsumes and critiques Beckett is, of course, that of modernist Formalism and its, in his view, exaggerated concern for form and technique. The one stylistic device that Lukács denounces most in formalist literature—with particular consideration of Beckett—is the stream of consciousness. While Lukács accuses many other modernist writers of the same charges and writes at greater length about for instance Kafka and Joyce, the criticism he directs at them is tempered by admissions of their literary skills: Kafka, he grants, possesses "extraordinary evocative power," and Joyce has "manifest abilities" as a writer. With regard to Beckett, however, he does not make any such concessions, as it is in his novels that Lukács identifies "perhaps the *ne plus ultra* of this [formalist] development," accusing him of presenting us "with an image of the utmost human degradation—an idiot's vegetative existence," an adoption of "perversity and idiocy as types of the *condition humaine*."[63]

Adorno, on the other hand, was, as is well known, a great admirer of Beckett. Not only is he the author of "Trying to understand Endgame," but, as Rolf Tiedemann has pointed out, it is also not exaggerated "to read behind every page of the *Aesthetic Theory*, which was to be dedicated to Beckett, an implicit discussion of Beckett's work," bearing witness to the "elective affinity" Adorno seems to have felt toward Beckett.[64] As much as Adorno's predilection for and writing on Beckett should be read as an element inherent to the Adornian philosophical project in its own right, it is also (and at the same time) to be seen as an explicit "counter-program" to Lukács.

Just as Lukács's understanding of realism, so does Adorno's respective conception take its form with reference to the notion of totality, that is, with reference to *his* reading of Hegel's infamous claim that "The True is the whole." To be sure: Other than Lukács, Adorno does *not* take the dictum as a *predictive* guideline that would instruct realist representation, but rather as a statement that has ultimately been invalidated by history itself—a statement that provides the ultimate evidence for the falseness of what he takes to be Hegel's overall identitarian system. As Adorno had already declared in his programmatic inaugural lecture:

> Whoever chooses philosophy as a profession today must first reject the illusion that earlier philosophical enterprises began

with: that the power of thought is sufficient to grasp the totality of the real. […] The crisis of idealism comes at the same time as a crisis in philosophy's pretension to totality. The *autonome ratio*—this was the thesis of every idealistic system—was supposed to be capable of developing the concept of reality, and in fact all reality, from out of itself. This thesis has disintegrated.[65]

Accordingly, Adorno parries Hegel's dictum with his by now equally notorious counter-dictum: "The whole is the false."[66] The task of realist literature that Adorno derives from this verdict is to make intelligible and perceptible precisely this pastness of any (idea of) totality, and it is in Beckett's literature that he recognizes the "pinnacle" of such a formal articulation, that is, the highpoint of "contemporary anti-art," which is the only art still worth being considered art *after* Auschwitz:[67]

> Beckett has given us the only fitting reaction to the situation of the concentration camp—a situation he never calls by name, as if it were subject to an image ban. What is, he says, is like a concentration camp.[68]

If the main charge Lukács brings against Beckett is that his literature merely portrays the consciousness of individual isolated beings and thus pretends that it is no longer possible to cognitively grasp society as a whole, paradoxically, Adorno agrees with Lukács on precisely this point, although he takes this fundamental position to be accurate and Beckett's literature to be an exact representation of the subjectively experienced fragmentation of social reality:

> These stumps of people, these people who have actually lost their "I", they are actually really the products of the world in which we live. It is not Beckett, who reduces for any speculative reasons; rather, to put it very pointedly, he is realistic in the sense that in these figures, which are at once stumps and something general, he is the precise interpreter of what individual human beings become as mere functions of the universal social context. He photographs, so to speak, the society in which everything is functional, from its miserable side, by showing what man becomes in this functional world.[69]

Contrary to Lukács, for Adorno, it is thus precisely Beckett's literary "depiction of ubiquitous regression" that has to be read as an accurate articulation of the "state of the world that so accommodates the law of regression that it no longer has anything to hold up against it."[70] What Lukács takes to be the loss of reality in modernist literature in general and in Beckett in particular, is precisely what for Adorno constitutes the very kernel of its and consequently Beckett's realism:

> Beckett is more realistic than the socialist realists who counterfeit reality by their very principle. If they took reality seriously enough they would eventually realize what Lukács condemned when during the days of his imprisonment in Romania he is reported to have said that he had finally realized that Kafka was a realist writer.[71]

To be precise, if Adorno does take Beckett's literature to be realist, he does not believe it to positively reproduce social reality. For Adorno,

Beckett's "narratives, which he sardonically calls novels, no more offer objective descriptions of social reality than—as the widespread misunderstanding supposes—they present the reduction of life to basic human relationships, that minimum of existence that subsists *in extremis*."[72] The blatant representation of "content" as such would constitute a relapse into a positivist and empirical illusion, which, from Adorno's perspective, is precisely what dialectical thinking is supposed to overcome and what he takes "Lukács' neo-naiveté" to be guilty of: The defense of and even demand for a literature that merely creates the false appearance of harmony and thus serves as the ideological counterpart of the general mystification, helping to legitimize the world as it is.[73] Thus, when Adorno nonetheless qualifies Beckett's literature as being realistic and asserts that his "novels do, however, touch on fundamental layers of experience *hic et nunc*," he does so because he believes them to incorporate the general contradictions of the world from which they emerge: "This shabby, damaged world of images is the negative imprint of the administered world. To this extent Beckett is realistic."[74]

---

Critically summarizing and condensing the two antagonistic positions in this debate about twentieth-century realism, we cannot but note a peculiar fact: As much as Adorno and Lukacs weigh Beckett's literary achievement in fundamentally opposite terms (the one emphasizing its content, the other its form), on a very elemental level, they ultimately and implicitly agree on a certain understanding of realism that remains within the confines of a reflection of social reality—the only difference being that Lukács takes its task to be a prescriptive and Adorno a descriptive one.[75] What is more, is that both philosophers read Beckett's literature in precisely these terms—again, the only difference being that Adorno takes Beckett's literature to be a precise portrayal of the impossibility of the social whole, that is, of its fragmentation, whereas Lukács sees in it a cementing of that very fragmentation that needs to be overcome.

As much as the two positions seem to have highly divergent accounts not only of totality but consequently also of realism, they ultimately *converge in their very divergence* and thus lead this (symptomatic) debate into a paradoxical impasse. It is precisely at this impasse—at the points of impossibility within the debate—at which one name can be found: namely, "Beckett." What does this emblematic name really stand for in the midst of this heated debate? Or, to ask this question with Badiou by way of altering a title of one of his books: "De quoi Beckett est-il le nom?"[76]

Taking up the previously elaborated structure of the Beckettian pseudocouple, we can phrase this question yet differently: What if Adorno and Lukács are really to be read as a Beckettian pseudocouple and their debate as a not yet written novel of Beckett, and what if *L'Innommable / The Unnamable* provides the method with which to read this peculiar text? "De quoi *L'Innommable* est-il le nom?" If, as Fredric Jameson put it, the debate leaves us with the peculiar impression that "each position is in some sense right and yet that neither is any longer wholly acceptable," could it be that it is precisely Beckett who, in his novel *L'Innommable / The Unnamable* gives form to the impossibility underlying this logical structure in spelling out the peculiar "unheeded neither"—the unnamable—at its center and, in doing so, shows us not only the Real of Realism but also of Dialectic itself?[77]

---

As is well known, Beckett's early writing of the 1930s and 1940s was deeply influenced by the work of his "master," James Joyce. Beckett was introduced to Joyce shortly after his arrival in Paris, where he soon became part of Joyce's inner circle, assisting him with various literary tasks, most notably with the preparation of *Work in Progress*, the project that was to become *Finnegans Wake*.[78] Right from the outset, Beckett was downright fascinated with Joyce—a sentiment that only grew stronger over time, up to the point of imitating Joyce's posture, holding his cigarette in a similarly mannered way, even wearing the same shoes and in the same size as Joyce, although it was obvious that they were far too small for Beckett's feet.[79] Above all, however, Joyce's influence showed in Beckett's writing and, in particular, in his early novels - a tendency, Beckett himself was only too well aware of, and, as one can gather from his early letters, was more than eager to let go. About his first novelistic attempt, *Dream of Fair to Middling Women*, he writes: "Of course it stinks of Joyce in spite of most earnest endeavors to endow it with my own odors," about a year later even taking a pledge to finally stop this stylistic emulation. "But I vow I will get over J.J. ere I die. Yessir."[80]

However, despite all of Beckett's early attempts to get out from under the long shadow of Joyce, *Murphy*, the first in the series of his novels, is still firmly rooted in the department of what Beckett called "Joyceology," full as it is of well-versed wordplays, bookish references, knowledgeable allusions, and sophisticated jokes.[81] It was only after the summer of 1945, when Beckett experienced what has become known as his "revelation," that he was finally able to develop a literary *method* (a way of *going forward*) different from the one adopted by Joyce—a method that, as he put it, consisted "in *subtracting* rather than *adding*."[82]

As Beckett points out, Joyce's novelistic project admittedly is one of *addition*, with Joyce continuously including, attaching, and appending ever more material to his texts, constantly multiplying and refining his myriad of references, allusions, and wordplays: an ever-growing material expansion on the level of the novel's form, leading to an ever-growing semantic expansion on the level of its content. While for years, Beckett had tried to imitate this Joycean (practice of a) "Work in Progress," it was only after his revelation that he was finally able to turn toward his own practice of a "work in regress": his literature of *subtraction* that instead of striving for an ever-growing material and semantic expansion, ventured down the opposite path, aiming for an ever-shrinking material and semantic contraction and confinement.[83]

Throughout Beckett's series of novels, this subtraction is evident, first and foremost, on the level of the novel's form. From *Mercier et Camier* onward, the previously excessive vocabulary and abundant references are being narrowed down to a minimum, giving way to what Beckett himself labeled as his "syntax of extreme weakness."[84] On this side of linguistic reduction, one also has to take into account Beckett's decision to no longer write directly in his mother tongue and instead to start writing in French—a decision he justified with his "need to be ill equipped"—"le besoin d'être mal armé."[85]

Next to this subtraction on the level of the novel's form, there is the subtraction of its content. From the very beginning of the series, Beckett's ever ongoing "creatures" display a tendency toward restriction and restraint—one only has to think of the series's opening scene, with Murphy tied up in his rocking chair. This tendency keeps increasing as the creatures move from relative mobility to successive immobility. Not only do their means and aids of transportation progressively disintegrate or disappear (the notorious bicycles or crutches), but so do the "creatures" themselves: physical capacities diminish and bodies disintegrate, limbs fail and even go missing. The characters proceed from walking to limping, from stumbling to crawling until they ultimately end up in a state of virtual immobility.

Where does this twofold—this doubled—reduction of form and content lead to? What happens at the point where it is impossible to subtract either side any further, when this movement reaches its necessary impasse—the point at which Beckett stumbles into the aforementioned literary impossibility, the, as he has it, "end of the jaunt," where "there being nobody left to utter and, independently perhaps, certainly superfluously, nothing left to utter about."[86] What do we end up with at the end of this ongoing going on of subtraction? When the novel's form and content, its narrator and narrated, language and body for that matter, have been reduced to the point of their paradoxical intersection?

What *The Unnamable* leaves us with at this paradoxical endpoint of subtraction is nothing but a voice that keeps telling itself: "It is solely a question of voices, no other image is appropriate."[87] In other words, what we encounter is the prosopopoeia of the novel itself – the point where all the novel does, is to tell its own telling, until all that is being told and all that is going on, is a sheer "going on" itself: "Keep going, going on, call that going, call that on."[88] This is a movement that Beckett once believed to detect in Joyce's work, but that rather provides us with a fitting description of his own literary endeavor: "Here form *is* content, content *is* form. [...] His writing is not *about* something; it is *that something itself.*"[89] While Joyce generates a hypertrophy of possibilities (and ultimately of possibilities of possibilities) of meaning, Beckett works toward the exploration of a specific formal impossibility of form (by means of form itself) – thus performing the formalization of the impasse of formalization of (realist) novel itself. By subtracting ever more – subtracting even the "sub-" of "subtraction" itself – ultimately, all we are left with is pure traction; the pure novelness of the novel, its drivenness as the sheer forward momentum of prose (*prorsus*).[90]

---

Where does all of this leave us with regard to the Beckettian pseudocouple of Lukács and Adorno? As we have seen, what we encounter in Beckett's *Unnamable* is not the depiction of a stream of consciousness, as both, Lukács and Adorno had taken it to be.

Rather, it confronts us with a novel that narrates itself, that takes its very own form as its content, and, in doing so, allows us to think the un-relation of this peculiar pseudocouple and its corresponding conceptualizations of realism.

If in Lukács's understanding, realism "must go on," as its task consists of a continual working towards totality and with it, towards an ever-receding, good end (of art) to come, Adorno, on the other hand, takes the task of literature to be the depiction of a lost totality, and thus the epitome of end that has already taken place: Art lives on because the moment of its realization was missed. In this understanding, the (realist) end (of art) amounts to art in the state of its afterlife – a post-apocalyptical state of "perennial crisis" – in which all it does is to endlessly repeat that, in fact, it "can't go on."[91] Even though the two positions seem to be directly contradicting one another, they nonetheless *converge in their divergence* in that both of them remain within the confines of what Hegel calls "bad infinity"—a necessarily endless maneuver, never able to reach its goal. What Beckett, however, might allow us to think is the dialectization of these two strands of (and most likely *within*) dialectics— a realism hinging on the impossible "going on" of an end of art that Hegel might as well have had in mind all along.

# Notes

1   Cf. Samuel Beckett, *Murphy*, ed. James C. C. Mays (London: Faber and Faber, 2009). To be precise: between 1931 and 1932 (and thus before *Murphy*), Beckett had already written a novel with the title *Dream of Fair*

*to Middling Women*. However, this novel remained unpublished during his lifetime, though serving as a "quarry" for Beckett's further literary endeavors (excerpts found their way into the collection *More Pricks than Kicks* (1934) and finally also into *Murphy*). For a summary of the publication history of this "very first" of Beckett's novels, (which was finally published after his death and can thus also be considered to be the "very last" ), cf. "Dream of Fair to Middling Women," in *The Grove Companion to Samuel Beckett*, ed. Chris J. Ackerley and Stanley E. Gontarski (New York: Grove Press, 2004), 150-2. Ackerley and Gontarski recognize *Dream of Fair to Middling Women* as "less a novel than scenes within a dream structure." Ibid., 151.

2   Paul Shields, "Pseudocouples" in Ackerley and Gontarski, *The Grove Companion to Samuel Beckett*, 463. For a discussion of the proliferation of all kinds of symmetrical configurations in *Murphy*, cf. Ruben Rabinovitz, "Murphy and the Uses of Repetition," in *The Development of Samuel Beckett's Fiction* (Urbana: University of Illinois Press, 1984), 71–103.

3   Ibid., 464. Cf. Samuel Beckett, *Watt*, ed. Chris J. Ackerley (London: Faber and Faber, 2009).

4   See Dolar's contribution to the present volume.

5   For instance, "I know creatures are supposed to have no secrets for their authors, but I'm afraid mine for me have little else." Samuel Beckett in a letter to Kay Boyle on October 7, 1961, in *The Letters of Samuel Beckett, Volume III: 1957–1965*, ed. George Craig, Martha Dow Fehsenfeld, Dan Gunn, and Lois More Overbeck (Cambridge: Cambridge University Press, 2014), 436.

6   On the connection between walking and writing as a fundamental methodological question of the realist novel, see Thomas Schestag's preface to the German translation of Balzac's *Théorie de la Démarche*: Thomas Schestag, "Piedestal," in Honoré de Balzac, *Theorie des Gehens*, trans. Alma Vallazza (Zürich: Edition Howeg, 1997), 7–67. Schestag shows that Balzac's *Théorie de la Démarche*, which is usually considered to be a marginal text of the *Comédie Humaine*, can just as well be read as its centerpiece—that is, as a presentation of the very method of the Balzacian project as such.

7   As indicated by the publication dates, Beckett's novel *Mercier et Camier* takes up a unique place in the series' chronological succession. Beckett wrote *Mercier et Camier* between July and October 1946 during what has become known as his "frenzy of writing," the period of immense creative output that followed his decision to write in French. *Mercier et Camier* thus represents Beckett's first novel written directly in French. Since, at the time, Beckett was not able to find a publisher for *Mercier et Camier*, the text remained unpublished for over twenty years. It was only after Beckett had won the Nobel Prize in 1969 and his publishers started asking for new

publishing material that *Mercier et Camier* retroactively took up its place in the series of novels. Beckett undertook its translation between 1970 and 1973, making for a gap of twenty-five years between the French writing and the English rewriting of the novel. For further information about the genesis, translation, and publication history cf. Knowlson, James, *Damned to Fame: The Life of Samuel Beckett* (London: Bloomsbury, 1990), 360pp, 574pp, as well as Seán Kennedy, "Preface," in Samuel Beckett, *Mercier and Camier*, ed. Seán Kennedy (London: Faber and Faber, 2010), vii–xi.

8   Samuel Beckett in a letter to George Reavy on May 14, 1947, in *The Letters Vol. II*, 55.

9   Samuel Beckett in a letter to Thomas MacGreevy on January 4, 1948, in *The Letters Vol. II*, 71.

10  Samuel Beckett in a letter to George Reavy on July 8, 1948, in *The Letters Vol. II*, 80.

11  It is essential to point out that while Beckett was pleased with the prospect of seeing the three novels collected in one volume, he repeatedly informed his publishers that he did not want the books to be titled a trilogy. As he wrote to his English publisher, John Calder: "Not 'Trilogy', I beseech you, just the three titles and nothing else." Samuel Beckett in a letter to John Calder on December 29, 1957, quoted after Ackerley and Gontarski, *The Grove Companion to Samuel Beckett*, 586. A year later, Beckett repeats: "I'm glad to have confirmation of your decision to publish the three in one. I can think of no general title. TRINITY would not do. It seems to me the three separate titles should be enough." Samuel Beckett in a letter John Calder on December 19, 1958, in *The Letters of Samuel Beckett, Vol. III*, 187. To his American publisher, Barney Rosset, Beckett writes: "Delighted to hear you are doing the 3 in 1 soon. Simply can't think, as I told Calder, of a general title and can't bear the thought of word trilogy appearing anywhere, what a hopeless unsatisfactory bastard I am. If it's possible to present the thing without either I'd be grateful." Samuel Beckett in a letter to Barney Rosset on May 5, 1959, in *The Letters Vol. III*, 230. To Jérôme Lindon of Minuit, Beckett merely makes the ironic remark: "They are proposing to publish M., M.M., et L'I. in a single volume. A dream, for my rheumatics." Samuel Beckett in a letter to Jérôme Lindon on November 11, 1956, in *The Letters Vol. II*, 672. To his longtime friend Barbara Bray he writes: "I was told the 3 in 1 was imminent. Please God he doesn't call it a trilogy." Samuel Beckett in a letter to Barbara Bray on March 26, 1959, in *The Letters Vol. III*, 222.

12  Samuel Beckett, *Molloy* (Paris: Les Éditions de Minuit, 1951), 9.

13  Samuel Beckett, *Molloy*, ed. Shane Weller (London: Faber and Faber, 2009). 4 [emphasis mine].

14  Beckett, *Murphy*, 7.

15  Samuel Beckett, *The Unnamable*, ed. Steven Connor (London: Faber and Faber, 2010), 1.

16  Ibid., 134.

17  Another indication that *L'Innommable* / *The Unnamable* indeed constitutes the series' paradoxical ending in precisely the sense insinuated above is that, admittedly, it would be wrong to simply speak of it as of Beckett's last novel. After all, we also have to consider *Comment C'est* (1961) / *How It Is* (1964), which, at least on the cover of the French – not the English – edition, is also designated as a novel. What makes it challenging to identify the genre of this particular text is, however, not only the inconsistent peritextual marking but rather its form itself. Since *Comment C'est* / *How It Is* is written without any punctuation marks and solely in lower-case letters, some readers have taken it to be not a prose work but rather a poem. Cf. for example Édouard Magessa O'Reilly, "Preface," in Samuel Beckett, *How It Is*, ed. Édouard Magessa O'Reilly (London: Faber and Faber 2009), xi. Other readers have, in turn, classified the text among Beckett's dramatic works and labeled it as a "dramatic monologue," since it needs to be read aloud and thus requires the spoken language to be understood on a semantic level. Ackerley and Gontarski, *The Grove Companion to Samuel Beckett*, 105. It appears as if it has to remain undecided whether *Comment C'est* / *How It Is* should be classified as a work of prose, poetry, or drama, or whether it represents a formal experiment within the form of the novel that ultimately leads to a transcendence of this very form within itself. There is, however, one essential feature that clearly distinguishes this text from the previous novels in the series, namely its title. Although the working title had been "Pim," Beckett ultimately decided against a proper name and opted for the wordplay "Comment C'est" / "How It Is." On the one hand side, this title insinuates that the text offers a registry of what has (already) happened and thus the ultimate protocol of "how it is." As the incipit goes: "how it was I quote before Pim with Pim after Pim how it is." Beckett, *How It Is*, 3. Viewed from this perspective, the title seems to allude to an ultimate endpoint – a point from which it is possible to draw an ultimate conclusion and thus to get the 'complete picture.' The French version of the title, however, phonetically also alludes to the verb 'commencer' (infinitive or imperative), which suggests that one is not only confronted with an end but (also) with a (new) beginning. Hence, the title itself encapsulates the particular antithesis in question: "one can't go on one goes on as before can one ever stop put a stop that's more like it one can't go on one can't stop put a stop," ibid., 78. Beckett's series of novels is thus a (potentially) open series not only with regards to its point of departure (cf. footnote 1) but also its end. As Beckett wrote to his

German publisher, Peter Suhrkamp: "This work is a complete whole only in so far as one takes for granted the impossibility of going on. That, alas, is my feeling, but one never knows. Just as one might locate the point of departure in Murphy." Samuel Beckett in a letter to Peter Suhrkamp on January 9, 1954, in *The Letters Vol. II*, 442.

18  Samuel Beckett in a letter to Thomas McGreevy on July 17, 1930, in *The Letters of Samuel Beckett, Volume I: 1929–1940*, ed. George Craig, Martha Dow Fehsenfeld, Dan Gunn, and Lois More Overbeck (Cambridge: Cambridge University Press, 2009), 26.

19  Samuel Beckett in a letter to Thomas McGreevy in August 1930, in *The Letters Vol. I*, 35.

20  Samuel Beckett in a letter to Thomas McGreevy on January 25, 1931, in *The Letters Vol. I*, 62.

21  Samuel Beckett in a letter to Thomas McGreevy on November 8, 1931, in *The Letters Vol. I*, 93.

22  Samuel Beckett in a letter to Thomas McGreevy on August 4, 1932, in *The Letters Vol. I*, 111.

23  Samuel Beckett in a letter to Aidan Higgins on August 30, 1955, in *The Letters Vol. II*, 544.

24  Ibid.

25  Samuel Beckett in a letter to Aidan Higgins on February 8, 1952, in *The Letters Vol. II*, 319.

26  Samuel Beckett in a letter to Jacoba Van Velde on February 19, 1952, in *The Letters Vol. II*, 321.

27  Samuel Beckett in a letter to Barney Rosset on August 21, 1954, in *The Letters Vol. II*, 497.

28  Samuel Beckett in a letter to Thomas McGreevy on December 14, 1953, in *The Letters Vol. II*, 434.

29  Samuel Beckett in "An Interview with Beckett," interview by Israel Shenker, in *Samuel Beckett: The Critical Heritage*, ed. Lawrence Graver and Raymond Federman (London/New York: Routledge and Kegan Paul, 2005), 163.

30  Samuel Beckett in a letter to Jacoba van Velde on December 15, 1956, in *The Letters Vol. II*, 686.

31  Samuel Beckett in a letter to Jacoba van Velde on September 27, 1956, in *The Letters Vol. II*, 658.

32  Samuel Beckett in a letter to Pamela Mitchell on September 28, 1956, in *The Letters Vol. II*, 658.

33  Samuel Beckett in a letter to Pamela Mitchell on March 12, 1956, in *The Letters Vol. II*, 606–7 [emphasis mine].

34  Samuel Beckett in a letter to Thomas McGreevy on July 30, 1956, in *The Letters Vol. II*, 640 [emphasis mine].

35  Samuel Beckett in a letter to Ethna MacCarthy on November 22, 1957, in *The Letters Vol. III*, 76 [emphasis mine].

36  Samuel Beckett in a letter to Jérôme Lindon on April 10, 1951, in *The Letters Vol. II*, 234.

37  Samuel Beckett in a letter to Jacoba Van Velde on February 19, 1952, in *The Letters Vol. II*, 321.

38  Samuel Beckett in a letter to Pamela Mitchell on June 23, 1954 in *The Letters Vol. II*, 487, FN 3.

39  Samuel Beckett in a letter to Barbara Bray on November 29, 1959, in *The Letters Vol. III*, 183.

40  Samuel Beckett in a letter to A. J. Leventhal on February 3, 1959, in *The Letters Vol. III*, 194.

41  Samuel Beckett in a letter to Barney Rosset on February 11, 1954, in *The Letters Vol. III*, 456–7.

42  Lawrence Shainberg, "Exorcising Beckett," *The Paris Review* 104 (1987).

43  Beckett, *The Unnamable*, 51.

44  Ibid., 3, 18, 14, 16, 5.

45  Ibid., 19.

46  Ibid., 7. It is interesting to note that, just as the novel *Mercier et Camier* only retroactively takes up its place in the series, the concept of the "pseudocouple" is only introduced as an afterthought, as evidenced by the manuscript of *L'Innommable*. Cf. Dirk van Hulle and Shane Weller, *The Making of Samuel Beckett's L'Innommable / The Unnamable* (London/Brussels: Bloomsbury/UPA, 2014), 107.

47  Ackerley and Gontarski, *The Grove Companion to Samuel Beckett*, 629.

48  As Beckett wrote in a letter to stage director Alan Schneider, who at the time was working on a production of *Endgame* in New York: "Hamm as stated, and Clov as stated, together as stated, nec tecum nec sine te, in such a place, and in such a world, that's all I can manage, more than I could." December

29, 1957 in *The Letters Vol. III*, 82. The classical quote can be traced back to either Ovid: "Sic ego nec sine te nec tecum vivere possum." (*Amores*, III, xi, 39.) or to Martial: "Nec tecum possum vivere nec sine te." (Epigram, XII, 46.)

49  Loraux, Nicole, "Le lien de la division," *Cahier du Collège Internationale de Philosophie* 4 (1987): 101–24. There is, of course, a theory of precisely this kind of non-relation. (Lacanian) Psychoanalysis shows us in what way the Real of (the sexual) difference is situated precisely in the very non-relation of the sexes: "Il n'y a pas de rapport sexuel." Jacques Lacan, *The Seminar, Book XX, Encore: On Feminine Sexuality and the Limits of Love and Knowledge, 1972-1973*, ed. Jacques-Alain Miller, trans. Bruce Fink (New York: W. W. Norton & Co., 1988).

50  On the question of totality within the tradition of what has become known as "Western Marxism" cf. Martin Jay, *Marxism and Totality: The Adventures of a Concept from Lukács to Habermas* (Berkeley/Los Angeles: University of California Press, 1984). For a discussion of Lukács cf. ibid., 81–127; and of Adorno cf. ibid., 241–75.

51  Not only did Adorno's philosophical position develop over long stretches through the confrontation with and recourse to Lukács—and can even be said to rest upon Lukács in its very genesis. But Lukács also frequently referred to Adorno, be it only to his position in explicit opposition to Adorno's. Thus, Lukács's project for a "Budapest School" of philosophy can be understood as a literal counter-project to the "Frankfurt School." For Lukács's remarks about the Budapest School and its position within a "world divided into two" cf. Georg Lukács, "Brief über die Budapester Schule," in *Autobiographische Texte und Gespräche*, *Werke*, vol. 18, ed. Frank Benseler and Werner Jung (Bielefeld: Aisthesis, 2005), 467. On the considerable influence of Lukács's work on the whole Adornian project cf. for example Gillian Rose, *The Melancholy Science: An Introduction to the Thought of Theodor W. Adorno* (London/New York: Verso, 2014), 45–55; Susan Buck-Morss, *The Origin of Negative Dialectics: Theodor W. Adorno, Walter Benjamin, and the Frankfurt Institute* (New York: The Free Press, 1977), 24pp, 45pp; Hammer, Espen, *Adorno and the Political* (London/New York: Routledge, 2005), 27–37.

52  For an outline of the Realism–Modernism–Debate cf. for example Rose, *The Melancholy Science*, 147–68.

53  Cf. Theodor W. Adorno in a letter to Giancarlo Fasano on July 16, 1961, quoted in Braunstein, Duckheim, "Adornos Lukács," 62.

54  Theodor W. Adorno, "Extorted Reconciliation: On Georg Lukács' *Realism in Our Time*," in *Notes to Literature*, vol. I, ed. Rolf Tiedemann, trans. Shierry Weber Nicholsen (New York: Columbia University Press, 1991), 217.

55  Adorno, "Extorted Reconciliation," 235.

56 Georg Lukács, "Preface [1962]," in *The Theory of the Novel: A Historico-philosophical Essay on the Forms of Great Epic Literature*, trans. Anna Bostock (London: Merlin Press, 1971), 22.

57 Theodor W. Adorno, "Graeculus (II). Notizen zu Philosophie und Gesellschaft 1943–1969," in *Frankfurter Adorno Blätter*, vol. VIII, ed. Rolf Tiedemann (München: edition text + kritik, 2003), 36 [my translation].

58 Georg Wilhelm Friedrich Hegel, *Phenomenology of Spirit*, trans. A. V. Miller (Oxford: Oxford University Press, 1977), 11.

59 Lukács, *History and Class Consciousness: Studies in Marxist Dialectics*, trans. Rodney Livingstone (Cambridge, MA: MIT Press, 1971), 198 [emphasis mine]. While it may seem that *History and Class Consciousness* has little to do with Lukács's later work on the aesthetics of literary realism, it nonetheless should be read as its veritable theoretical foundation. For it is here that Lukács seeks to demonstrate the extent to which an insight into totality is possible in the first place – namely through the solution of the Kantian dilemma by what he takes to be a "proletarian epistemology." Cf. Fredric Jameson, "The Case for Georg Lukács," in *Marxism and Form: Twentieth-Century Dialectical Theories of Literature*, ed. Georg Lukács (Princeton, NJ: Princeton University Press, 1974), 182–90. For a reading of *History and Class Consciousness* with regard to the question of its contemporary relevance cf. Slavoj Žižek, "From History and Class Consciousness to the Dialectic of Enlightenment … and Back," *New German Critique* 81 (2000): 107–32.

60 Lukács, *The Meaning of Contemporary Realism*, trans. John and Necke Mander (London: Merlin Press, 1963), 17.

61 Ibid., 20.

62 Ibid., 27.

63 Ibid., 45, 18, 31, 32. Lukács saw his reading of Beckett supported by the at the time prevailing existentialist reception, which led him to underpin his harsh judgment with a quotation from French critic Maurice Nadeau: "enveloped in eternal nothingness, we are no more than bubbles that burst on the surface of a muddy pool, producing that faint sound we call existence. […] with Beckett, triumphant nihilism penetrates into the work of art itself, dissolving the thing it creates into a fog of meaninglessness." Ibid., 66.

64 Rolf Tiedemann, "'Gegen den Trug der Frage nach dem Sinn'. Eine Dokumentation zu Adornos Beckett-Lektüre," in *Frankfurter Adorno Blätter*, vol. III, ed. Rolf Tiedemann (München: edition text + kritik, 1994), 18 [my translation]. On Adorno's intention to dedicate his *Aesthetic Theory* to Beckett cf. the editorial afterword in Theodor W. Adorno, *Aesthetic Theory*,

ed. Gretel Adorno and Rolf Tiedemann, trans. Robert Hullot-Kentor (London/New York: Bloomsbury, 2013), 483.

65  Theodor W. Adorno, "The Actuality of Philosophy," *Telos: Critical Theory of the Contemporary* 31, no. 120 (1977): 120–1.

66  Theodor W. Adorno, *Minima Moralia: Reflections on a Damaged Life*, trans. E. F. N. Jephcott (London/New York: Verso, 2005), 50.

67  Adorno, *Aesthetic Theory*, 365.

68  Theodor W. Adorno, *Negative Dialectics*, trans. E. B. Ashton (New York/London: Continuum, 2007), 380.

69  Adorno in, Theodor W. Adorno, Walter Boehlich, Martin Esslin, Hans-Geert Falkenberg, and Ernst Fischer, "'Optimistisch zu denken ist kriminell' Eine Fernsehdiskussion über Samuel Beckett," in *Frankfurter Adorno Blätter*, vol. III, ed. Rolf Tiedemann (München: edition text + kritik, 1994), 90pp [my translation].

70  Theodor W. Adorno, "Trying to Understand Endgame," in *Notes to Literature*, vol. I, ed. Rolf Tiedemann, trans. Shierry Weber Nicholsen (New York: Columbia University Press, 1991), 248.

71  Adorno, *Aesthetic Theory*, 423. On the anecdote about Lukács's Kafkaesk experience cf. also Adorno, "Graeculus (II)," 29.

72  Adorno, *Aesthetic Theory*, 42.

73  Adorno, "Extorted Reconciliation," 235. Adorno's remarks are, however, not without a certain irony: When he accuses Lukács of being blind to the political system and declares him to be nothing but "a person who rattles in his chains hopelessly, imagining that their clanking is the march of the *Weltgeist*," we have to keep in mind that it is Adorno who published this very text in a journal that (presumably without his knowing) was being financed by the CIA. Ibid., 239. Cf. Theodor Adorno, Walter Benjamin, Ernst Bloch, Bertolt Brecht, and Georg Lukács, *Aesthetics and Politics*, with an afterword by Fredric Jameson (London/New York: Verso, 1980), 143.

74  Adorno, *Aesthetic Theory*, 42, 43.

75  As has already been highlighted by Fredric Jameson: "To be sure, some of Adorno's most remarkable analyses […] document his assertion that the greatest modern art, even the most apparently un- or anti-political, in reality holds a mirror to the 'total system' of late capitalism. Yet, in retrospect, this now seems a most unexpected revival of a Lukács-type 'reflection theory' of aesthetics, under the spell of a political and historical despair that plagues both houses and finds praxis henceforth unimaginable."Fredric Jameson, "Reflections in Conclusion," in *Aesthetics and Politics*, ed. Theodor W.

Adorno, Walter Benjamin, Ernst Bloch, Bertolt Brecht, and Georg Lukács (London/New York: Verso, 2007), 208.

76  Cf. Alain Badiou, *De quoi Sarkozy est-il le nom?* (Paris: Lignes, 2007). To identify the realism-debate as a symptom (of the twentieth century) is to identify it as an effect of a certain symbolically structured (Real) impasse, that is, as a site, where this impasse is played out and repeated in a way that produces some "impossible" satisfaction (enjoyment). For a general account of the twentieth century in view of its symptomatic relation to this (real) impasse cf. Alain Badiou, *The Century*, trans. Alberto Toscano (Cambridge/Malden, MA: Polity Press, 2007).

77  Jameson, "Reflections in Conclusion," 196. Samuel Beckett, "Neither," in *Texts for Nothing and Other Shorter Prose 1950–1976*, ed. Mark Nixon (London: Faber and Faber, 2010), 167. The reason for which it can only be a *novel* that can shed light on this impasse that is the formalization of realist literature—that can formalize this (real) impasse of formalization—is not only the inherent connection between the novel and realism. (As Jameson put it: "It does seem to me that it would be very difficult to discuss either realism or 'the novel' in any satisfactory way without also ending up in a discussion of the other." Fredric Jameson, "Antinomies of the Realism-Modernism Debate," *Modern Language Quarterly* 73, no. 3 [2012]: 476.) It also has to do with the inherent connection between the novel and totality, indicated notably by a text of the young Lukács, namely, his *Theory of the Novel*. For an extensive reading of the un-relation between Lukács and Adorno that enters the debate from its edges, from its historical margins as it were, by bringing together Lukács's *Theory of the Novel* with Adorno's posthumously published "Notes on The Unnamable" cf. Eva Heubach, *The Real of Realism: Samuel Beckett's "L'Innommable / The Unnamable"* [forthcoming].

78  On Beckett's involvement with *Finnegans Wake* and his relation to Joyce cf. Knowlson, *Damned to Fame*, 97pp.

79  Cf. Ackerley and Gontarski, *The Grove Companion to Samuel Beckett*, 286.

80  Samuel Beckett in a letter to Charles Prentice on August 15, 1931, in *The Letters Vol. I*, 81; Samuel Beckett in a letter to Samuel Putnam on June 28, 1932, in *The Letters Vol. I*, 108.

81  Samuel Beckett in a letter to Niall Montgomery on December 12, 1960, in *The Letters Vol. II*, 209.

82  Samuel Beckett in an interview with James Knowlson in 1956, quoted in Knowlson, *Damned to Fame*, 352 [emphasis mine]. On Beckett's "revelation," the experience that led to what has become known as his "frenzy of writing" (the immense production of work between 1945 and 1949), cf. Knowlson, *Damned to Fame*, 351pp. In an interview with Gabriel D'Aubarède Beckett

connected this pivotal moment to the "birth" of his creatures: "Molloy and the others came to me the day I became aware of my own folly." Quoted in *Samuel Beckett: The Critical Heritage*, 217.

83  On the question of confinement cf. James Little, *Samuel Beckett in Confinement: The Politics of Closed Space* (London/New York: Bloomsbury, 2019).

84  Beckett repeatedly mentioned this expression in his letters. To his friend Barbara Bray he writes about his work on the radio play "Embers": "I'm struggling along with the new moan, trying to find the rhythm and syntax of extreme weakness, penury perhaps I should say. Sometimes I think I'm getting on, then realise how far I am from it still." Samuel Beckett in a letter to Barbara Bray on March 11, 1959, in *The Letters Vol. III*, 211.

85  Samuel Beckett in a letter to Hans Naumann on February 17, 1954, in *The Letters Vol. II*, 462, 464. On an earlier occasion, Beckett gives the following explanation: "Samuel Beckett is a Dublin poet and novelist who, after long years of residence in France had adopted the French language as his working medium. Invited to give some account of his reasons for now writing in French, rather than this [sic] native language, […] he confessed at last in a strong or rather weak Dublin accent: '*Pour faire remarquer moi*.'" "Notes on Contributors," *Transition* 2 (1948): 146–7. It was only after having disremembered his mother tongue to a sufficient degree that he felt like taking it up again in his writing practice: "now that I've forgotten half my English I feel like going back to it." Samuel Beckett in a letter to Kay Boyle on July 26, 1957, in *The Letters Vol. III*, 56.

86  Samuel Beckett in a letter to Aidan Higgins on February 8, 1952, in *The Letters Vol. II*, 319. Beckett continues: "These are hindrances to one deficient in the professional outlook." Ibid.

87  Beckett, *The Unnamable*, 61. On the question of the voice in Beckett cf. Mladen Dolar, "Nothing Has Changed," in *Beckett and Nothing: Trying to Understand Beckett*, ed. Daniela Caselli (Manchester/New York: Manchester University Press, 2010), 48–64; cf. also Llewelyn Brown, *Beckett, Lacan and the Voice* (Suttgart: ibidem, 2016).

88  Beckett, *The Unnamable*, 1.

89  Samuel Beckett, "Dante … Bruno. Vico.. Joyce," in *Disjecta: Miscellaneous Writings and a Dramatic Fragment*, ed. Ruby Cohn (New York: Grove Press, 1984), 27.

90  On this self-reflexive movement from subtraction to pure traction cf. Rebecca Comay and Frank Ruda, *The Dash—The Other Side of Absolute Knowing* (Cambridge, MA: MIT Press, 2018), 102.

91  Eva Geulen, *The End of Art: Readings in a Rumour after Hegel*, trans. James McFarland (Stanford, CA: Stanford University Press, 2006).

# Bibliography

Ackerley, Chris J., and Stanley E. Gontarski. *The Grove Companion to Samuel Beckett*. New York: Grove Press, 2004.
Adorno, Theodor W. "The Actuality of Philosophy." *Telos: Critical Theory of the Contemporary* 31, no. 120 (1977): 120–33.
Adorno, Theodor W. "Extorted Reconciliation: On Georg Lukács' *Realism in Our Time*." In *Notes to Literature*, vol. I, edited by Rolf Tiedemann, translated by Shierry Weber Nicholsen, 216–40. New York: Columbia University Press, 1991.
Adorno, Theodor W. "Trying to Understand Endgame." In *Notes to Literature*, vol. I, edited by Rolf Tiedemann, translated by Shierry Weber Nicholsen, 241–75. New York: Columbia University Press, 1991.
Adorno, Theodor W. *Aesthetic Theory*, edited by Gretel Adorno and Rolf Tiedeman, translated by Robert Hullot-Kentor. London/New York: Continuum, 1997.
Adorno, Theodor W. "Graeculus (II). Notizen zu Philosophie und Gesellschaft 1943–1969." In *Frankfurter Adorno Blätter*, vol. VIII, edited by Rolf Tiedemann, 9–41. München: edition text + kritik, 2003.
Adorno, Theodor W. *Minima Moralia: Reflections on a Damaged Life*, translated by Edmund Jephcott. London/New York: Verso, 2005.
Adorno, Theodor W. *Negative Dialectics*, translated by E. B. Ashton. New York/London: Continuum, 2007.
Adorno, Theodor W., Walter Boehlich, Martin Esslin, Hans-Geert Falkenberg, and Ernst Fischer. "'Optimistisch zu denken ist kriminell' Eine Fernsehdiskussion über Samuel Beckett." In *Frankfurter Adorno Blätter*, vol. III, edited by Rolf Tiedemann, 78–122. München: edition text + kritik, 1994.
Adorno, Theodor W., Walter Benjamin, Ernst Bloch, Bertolt Brecht, and Georg Lukacs. *Aesthetics and Politics*, with an afterword by Fredric Jameson. London/New York: Verso, 2007.
Badiou, Alain. *De quoi Sarkozy est-il le nom?* Paris: Lignes, 2007.
Badiou, Alain. *The Century*, translated by Alberto Toscano. Cambridge/Malden, MA: Polity Press, 2007.
Badiou, Alain. *À la recherche du réel perdu*. Paris: Fayard, 2015.
Beckett, Samuel. *Molloy*. Paris: Les Éditions de Minuit, 1951.
Beckett, Samuel. "Dante … Bruno. Vico.. Joyce." In *Disjecta: Miscellaneous Writings and a Dramatic Fragment*, edited by Ruby Cohn, 18–23. New York: Grove Press, 1984.

Beckett, Samuel. *The Letters of Samuel Beckett, Volume I: 1929–1940*, edited by George Craig, Dow Fehsenfeld, Dan Gunn, and Lois More Overbeck. Cambridge: Cambridge University Press, 2009.
Beckett, Samuel. *Molloy*, edited by Shane Weller. London: Faber and Faber, 2009.
Beckett, Samuel. *Murphy*, edited by James C. C. Mays. London: Faber and Faber, 2009.
Beckett, Samuel. *Watt*, edited by Chris J. Ackerley. London: Faber and Faber, 2009.
Beckett, Samuel. "Neither." In *Texts for Nothing and Other Shorter Prose 1950–1976*, edited by Mark Nixon, 165–7. London: Faber and Faber, 2010.
Beckett, Samuel. *The Unnamable*, edited by Steven Connor. London: Faber and Faber, 2010.
Beckett, Samuel. *The Letters of Samuel Beckett, Volume II: 1941–1956*, edited by George Craig, Martha Dow Fehsenfeld, Dan Gunn, and Lois More Overbeck. Cambridge: Cambridge University Press, 2011.
Beckett, Samuel. *The Letters of Samuel Beckett, Volume III: 1957–1965*, edited by George Craig, Martha Dow Fehsenfeld, Dan Gunn, and Lois More Overbeck. Cambridge: Cambridge University Press, 2014.
Braunstein, Dirk and Simon Duckheim. "Adornos Lukács: Ein Lektürebericht." *Jahrbuch der Internationalen Lukács-Gesellschaft* 14, no. 15 (2014/2015): 27–86.
Brown, Llewellyn. *Beckett, Lacan and the Voice*. Stuttgart: ibidem, 2016.
Buck-Morss, Susan. *The Origin of Negative Dialectics: Theodor W. Adorno, Walter Benjamin, and the Frankfurt Institute*. New York: The Free Press, 1977.
Bürger, Peter. "Verschüttete Spuren. Georg Lukács in der Frankfurter Schule." *Neue Rundschau* 3 (2003): 163–73.
Comay, Rebecca and Frank Ruda. *The Dash—The Other Side of Absolute Knowing*. Cambridge, MA: MIT Press, 2018.
Dolar, Mladen. *A Voice and Nothing More*. Cambridge, MA: MIT Press, 2006.
Dolar, Mladen. "Nothing Has Changed." In *Beckett and Nothing: Trying to Understand Beckett*, edited by Daniela Caselli, 48–64. Manchester/New York: Manchester University Press, 2010.
Geulen, Eva. *The End of Art: Readings in a Rumour after Hegel*, translated by James McFarland. Stanford, CA: Stanford University Press, 2006.
Graver, Lawrence and Raymond Federman, edited by *Samuel Beckett: The Critical Heritage*. London/New York: Routledge and Kegan Paul, 2005.
Hammer, Espen. *Adorno and the Political*. London/New York: Routledge, 2005.
Hegel, Georg Wilhelm Friedrich. *Phenomenology of Spirit*, translated by A. V. Miller. Oxford: Oxford University Press, 1977.
Jameson, Fredric. "The Case for Georg Lukács." In *Marxism and Form: Twentieth-Century Dialectical Theories of Literature*, 182–90. Princeton, NJ: Princeton University Press, 1974.
Jameson, Fredric. "Reflections in Conclusion." In *Aesthetics and Politics*, with an afterword by Fredric Jameson, edited by Theodor W. Adorno, Walter Benjamin, Ernst Bloch, Bertolt Brecht, and Georg Lukács, 196–213. London/New York: Verso, 2007.

Jameson, Fredric. "Antinomies of the Realism-Modernism Debate." *Modern Language Quarterly* 73 (2012): 475–85.
Jay, Martin. *Marxism and Totality: The Adventures of a Concept from Lukács to Habermas* Berkeley/Los Angeles: University of California Press, 1984.
Kennedy, Seán. "Preface." In Samuel Beckett, *Mercier and Camier*, edited by Seán Kennedy, vii–xi. London: Faber and Faber, 2010.
Knowlson, James. *Damned to Fame: The Life of Samuel Beckett*. London: Bloomsbury, 1990.
Lacan, Jacques. *The Seminar. Book XX. Encore: On Feminine Sexuality and the Limits of Love and Knowledge. 1972–1973*, edited by Jacques-Alain Miller, translated by Bruce Fink. New York: W. W. Norton & Co., 1988.
Lacan, Jacques. *Le Séminaire. Livre XVIII. D'un discours qui ne serait pas du semblant. 1971*, edited by Jacques-Alain Miller. Paris: Seuil, 2006.
Little, James. *Samuel Beckett in Confinement: The Politics of Closed Space*. London/New York: Bloomsbury, 2019.
Loraux, Nicole. "Le lien de la division." *Cahier du Collège Internationale de Philosophie* 4 (1987): 101–24.
Lukács, Georg. *The Meaning of Contemporary Realism*, translated by John and Necke Mander. London: Merlin Press, 1963.
Lukács, Georg. *Realism in Our Time: Literature and the Class Struggle*, translated by John and Necke Mander. New York: Harper and Row, 1964.
Lukács, Georg. *History and Class Consciousness*, translated by Rodney Livingstone. Cambridge, MA: MIT Press, 1971.
Lukács, Georg. "Preface [1962]." In *The Theory of the Novel: A Historico-philosophical Essay on the Forms of Great Epic Literature*, translated by Anna Bostock, 11–22. London: Merlin Press, 1971.
Lukács, Georg. "Brief über die Budapester Schule." In *Autobiographische Texte und Gespräche, Werke*, vol. 18, edited by Frank Benseler and Werner Jung, 467–9. Bielefeld: Aisthesis, 2005.
Magessa O'Reilly, Édouard. "Preface." In Samuel Beckett. *How It Is*, edited by Édouard Magessa O'Reilly, vii–xv. London: Faber and Faber, 2009.
Rabinovitz, Ruben. "Murphy and the Uses of Repetition." In *The Development of Samuel Beckett's Fiction*, 71–103. Urbana: University of Illinois Press, 1984.
Rose, Gillian. *The Melancholy Science: An Introduction to the Thought of Theodor W. Adorno*. London/New York: Verso, 2014.
Schestag, Thomas. "Piedestal." In Honoré de Balzac. *Theorie des Gehens*, translated by Alma Vallazza, 7–67. Zürich: Edition Howeg, 1997.
Shields, Paul. "Pseudocouples." In *The Grove Companion to Samuel Beckett*, edited by Chris J. Ackerley and Stanley E. Gontarski, 43–465. New York: Grove Press, 2004.
Tiedemann, Rolf. "'Gegen den Trug der Frage nach dem Sinn'. Eine Dokumentation zu Adornos Beckett-Lektüre." In *Frankfurter Adorno Blätter*,

vol. III, edited by Rolf Tiedemann, 18–22. München: edition text + kritik, 1994.

Van Hulle, Dirk and Shane Weller. *The Making of Samuel Beckett's L'Innommable / The Unnamable*. London/Brussels: Bloomsbury/UPA, 2014.

Žižek, Slavoj. "From History and Class Consciousness to the Dialectic of Enlightenment … and Back." *New German Critique* 81 (2000): 107–32.

# VI

# *Watt* Forms Life: Beckett and the Theory of the Novel

## Philipp Weber

The following discussion aims to explore the relevance of the theory of the novel in the case of Samuel Beckett's early poetics. As is well established, the modern novel and its theory arise simultaneously in the times of the eighteenth century.[1] It is the novel's main aim to present life in the most appropriate manner, and therefore its theory is also a theory of life. The novel thus has to deal with the contradictive ensemble of form and life. In this context, Beckett goes one step further. His work can be understood as a confrontation with the novel's very own conditions. His poetics follow, thereby, a strategy of subtraction: they disassemble plot, figures, tropes, metaphors, sceneries, and even their rhetoric material. And they do the same with the entire genre of the novel. In the context of the theory of the novel, the early work of Samuel Beckett thus highlights a certain problem: his novel *Watt* published in 1953 can be regarded as standing in the direct genealogy of the novel's ensemble of form and life but, at the same time, as a self-directed subtraction to the bones.

To unfold the complex of the poetics of form and life in Beckett's novel *Watt*, the discussion will proceed as follows: *first*, it will reconsider the problem of the historical theorization of the novel. The connection between the modern novel and the concept of form and life is treated as the major foci of the argument. The novel can, however, not only be explained with reference to the concepts of form and life. They show that subjectivity is a certain instance of self-reflection, which elaborates a fundamental self-differentiation in the form of life and can accordingly be defined as a radically autonomous form. *Secondly*, the discussion will trace the impact that subjectivity has on the novel and how this relates to the concept of the death drive. This psychoanalytic term can be used to clarify certain aspects of subjectivity and its relation to the symbolic order. This will lead to the insight that the novel is the very modern poetic procedure of the subject's act of consciousness. *Thirdly*, the analysis will focus on Samuel Beckett's novel *Watt* with regard to the theorization of the novel. This will help to show that the novel *Watt* can be seen as a confrontation with its own genre and with the complex of form and life. The function of subjectivity in Beckett's poetics still acts as the very form of the novel but displays an excessive demand to question its own condition. As a *last point*, this specific feature of Beckett's poetics will be understood as the function of the death drive. The novel's character not only shows certain aspects of compulsive behavior but also fulfills such drives in its syntactical structure and in its framings. *Watt* marks the minimal difference in the life-form of subjectivity by subtracting it to its inner core.

## The Complex of Form and Life

It is the novel's heterogeneous nature that renders it difficult to define its precise "form." A major reason for the difficulties is the lack of poetological definitions of the novel: the novel knows no form, except the one it gives itself, but it is nevertheless able to gather and incorporate other minor forms (e.g., poems, songs). It thus appears to be an organic process of forms, and one might argue that there is no need for a kind of theory to align the modern novel, but instead one requires a theory of life to comprehend it.[2] For theorists and poets like Friedrich von Blankenburg and later, the European Romantics, life finds its adequate representation in the novel's way—or as Novalis puts it: "A novel is a life—as a book."[3] "With the (modern) novel," Rüdiger Campe claims, "literary form becomes a matter no longer of poetical forms but of the form of life."[4] Not only is the novel able to capture life in its processuality, even its representation itself becomes vivid and, in this sense, comes alive.[5] The modern novel thus produces an excess of forms, which not only pursues a single but two-folded aim: to bring life into a form and to bring its form into life. To this end, the novel, therefore, gathers certain strategies and techniques to "deal with life." So, while the understanding of the modern novel as a construct of form and life provides helpful insights in the genesis of the literary genre, it still needs to be clarified what the specific character of the form of life is that the novel is about.[6] Not only is the modern novel able to give answers with reference to a knowledge of life, and the inner connection between life and form, it also highlights different aspects of life that can only be described as the specific modi of subjectivity.[7] It is, therefore, necessary to clarify the connection between the novel and the form of life that it is dealing with: "subjectivity."

The Cartesian revolution of the *cogito* can be defined as the starting point for the development of modern subjectivity.[8] The subject displays a sort of self-questioning and doubting instance that is at the same time the indefeasible requirement of autonomous thinking and the crucial epistemic principle of modern times. However, its self-referential and negative structure dismisses the notion of any positive order of things or, to be more precise, the classic concept of the cosmos. It is Kant who takes the crucial step of destroying the concept of a closed and complete cosmos.[9] The ontological consistency of the world, so his first *Critique* shows, leads to a collapse within modern subjectivity: on the one hand Kant argues, "I always have the world-whole only in concept, but by no means as a whole in intuition," and on the other hand, the concept of this world-whole turns out to be a regress that "goes to infinity."[10] So there is no way to come across an absolute starting or endpoint, which nevertheless would be necessary for an adequate understanding of the world-whole.[11] The concept of a closed world thus displays an inner contradiction, and in turn, subjectivity has to acknowledge this contradiction to reach its own identity.

However, the outcome of the cosmological antinomies not only regards ontological and epistemological structures isolated from each other, but also affects modern poetics. One can argue that the modern novel is the decisive place where modern subjectivity comes to being and finds itself distinguished from the antique idea of a positive order of things. Georg Lukács stresses this aspect in his *Theory of the Novel* from 1916:

> The circle within which the Greeks led their metaphysical life was smaller than ours: that is why we cannot, as part of our life, place ourselves inside it. Or rather, the circle whose closed nature was the transcendental essence of their life has, for us, been broken; we cannot breathe in a closed world.[12]

In this passage, Lukács explains his view of the novel and how it emerges from the end of totality of the Greek epic. While every single thing has its defined and allocated place in the epic, the novel abolishes this cosmic closeness: "Kant's starry firmament," so goes the assumption, "now shines only in the dark night of pure cognition, it no longer lights any solitary wanderer's path."[13] The Kantian destruction of the cosmos is the explicit requirement of the emerging modern subjectivity—and by this the novel finds its form of definition. To abbreviate, "the central problem of the novel," Lukács states, is "to write off the closed and total forms which stem from a rounded totality of being."[14]

But what does the novel offer as a substitute? Well, at first glance, not much more than the advice "to go on with life." Therefore, the novel stands in close relation to the genre of biography but at the same time, articulates a decisive differentiation.[15] It is not only the forming of life as a biography that builds the novel's purpose, but it also shows that the *bios* is not willing to transform steadily into a *graphein*. Instead, life causes a differentiation-in-form that is rooted in a realm that is located precisely *in-between* the two. Psychoanalysis, in contrast, defines the necessary term for this realm in-between, which is neither natural nor cultural but establishes this difference in the first place. This is the death drive.

## The Subject's Death Drive

The term "death drive" has caused, from its first annunciation by Sigmund Freud up until today, some fatal misunderstandings and contradictions. Not least, this is due to its almost metaphysical relevance for the early forms of psychoanalysis and its resulting condemnation in the discipline. In recent times though, several authors have demanded a philosophical revision of the term.[16] Still, using the term "death drive" in the context of the theory of the novel (and in the following for the poetics of Beckett) may help with clarifying a specific moment of negativity and disruption of the subject, which is thought to be substantial in modern poetics.

Sigmund Freud first mentions the term "death drive" in his essay *Beyond the Pleasure Principle* from 1920. The drive operates as an opposing force to the until then sole drive of libido.[17] Freud detects a specific form of compulsion in the subject (through all steps of development) aiming to restore an "inorganic" status.[18]

Next to the libidinal drive, there has to be, so goes his theorizing, a radical deviant gain of pleasure, longing for destruction of life that manifests as a repetitive automatism. Such an automatism appears through a child's play as well as in the "compulsion to repeat" (the "Wiederholungszwang") of the neurotic.[19]

Jacques Lacan departs at this point from Freud's argumentation and shows the death drive's relation to the level of the signifier.[20] On the one hand, he sees the death drive as a universal foundation of the symbolic order, stating that "it is articulated at a level that can only be defined as a function of the signifying chain."[21] On the other hand, Lacan claims that the death drive is the inner core of *every* drive, it is their inner-most but concealed vividness. According to Lacan, "every drive is virtually a death drive," operating as an endless and repetitive excess.[22] The death drive is an explicitly "human" drive as it exists in the dimension of the symbolic order, and it is not so much a metaphysical principle in the form of a wanting of death. Instead, it is more like an indelible propulsion of the vividness of the subject.

Referring to Freud and Lacan but aiming for a more subject-philosophical resumption, Slavoj Žižek eventually speaks of the death drive as an "empty frame" in which the narrative of a subject is built.[23] Following Žižek, this kind of drive must be understood as "the Monstrous of a spontaneity not yet bound by any Law—in Freudian terms: of death drive."[24] With the death drive, the subject is able to represent itself in a unit outside of its natural and seemingly naïve being, namely, as a signifier in a symbolic order, which in turn is experienced as fundamental alienation: "the verbal sign that stands for the subject, that is, in which the subject posits itself as self-identical, bears the mark of an irreducible dissonance."[25] The death drive marks a gap between nature and culture as it just opens up a frame wherein the subject may be built:

> The key point is thus that the passage from "nature" to "culture" is not direct, that one cannot account for it within a continuous evolutionary narrative: something has to intervene between the two, a kind of "vanishing mediator", which is neither Nature nor Culture—this In-between is silently presupposed in all evolutionary narratives.[26]

Žižek's approach toward the death drive offers the chance to clarify its conceptual relationship to subjectivity: the death drive is the irreplaceable condition of a subject but barely visible and inacceptable for the *logos*. The break of the subject with the natural order cannot establish a coherent narrative of its being, yet it forces a subsequent reconfiguration. The form of life that is the subject does not gain its form by entering the natural order but by denying it. It does so in an act of consciousness that is connected to an inherent counterpart of life.

The inner excess of the form of life, by which it dismisses any other form than the one it gives itself, can now be defined as that of a death drive. A further helpful assumption might then be, that it is precisely this inherent excess, which is transformed into an aesthetic decision within the modern novel. In its giving-of-form, the novel conserves and fixes life, making it thus formable and representative in a symbolic order. The thing that is needed to bring the novel to its self-given form has to be defined as that of the subject's certain modus of negativity, which in turn is the death drive.[27]

While the theory of the novel has its specific issues when dealing with this complex, one can find a more intense confrontation within the novels themselves. In this sense, there might be no more radical author in explicating the dialectics of this specific problem of the novel than Samuel Beckett. As a matter of fact, it can be argued that in *Watt*, one can find the very point where the interaction of the two interrelated concepts of the novel, namely, form and life, are brought to their highest level of contradiction.[28]

## Form and Life in *Watt*

Samuel Beckett wrote his novel *Watt* during the times of the Second World War—between 1941 and 1945.[29] It is his first novel following his trip to Germany and certain characteristics of his diary can be found in the structure of the text.[30] Although these historic circumstances bring up the problem of the form of life in different and sensitive issues, we will limit the discussion to the topic of the poetic tradition of the novel.[31] At that time, however, the theory of the novel does not yet offer any new solutions to the problem that the complex of form and life produces.[32] The following reading of *Watt* will thus be bisected, taking into account formal aspects of the novel as well as ones relating to content. So, on the one hand, we have to deal with the form of life that the novel presents. On the other hand, we have to focus on the novel *Watt* as an "exemplar" of its own genre, referring to the question of the form of the novel itself.

As mentioned above, the novel is defined as a literary genre that includes different minor forms but lacks concrete poetological definitions. Hence, there is no doubt that *Watt* is a showpiece of a novel in this respect: through the whole book, the plot is complemented by poems, letters, songs (including notes), and shorter separated stories. Not only is *Watt* entitled as a novel, but it also does extensive work to proof this on the formal level. The formal aspect might serve as a first indication for the very strict boundary that surrounds the tradition of the novel. But this is not just an exercise of formal integration; it also sticks to the tradition merely by having the title it has, namely, *Watt*. *Watt* here stands next to a range of novels, that is the *Bildungsroman*. With the *Bildunsgroman*, the tradition of the novel changes in such a way that the title no longer simply refers to its main character but to subjectivity as such (e.g., *Wilhelm Meister*, *Hyperion* as well as *Tom Jones*, *Emile*, or *Jane Eyre*).[33] But while the titles of these novels disclose their implicit subject, *Watt* enfolds a difference in here: the novel does not only deal with the novel's character Watt, it also picks out the character's connection or even the knot that ties him to his master Mr. Knott (or more precisely to the household of Mr. Knott, where he works for an unspecified period as a manservant). Within the novel, we can find a certain form of domination that also affects the forming of life. *Watt* deals with "the entire body of Watt's experience, from the moment of his entering Mr. Knott's establishment to the moment of his leaving it."[34] The earlier and later perspectives do not change this constellation, which is the very centerpiece of the novel: here, the form of the narrated life of Watt is in coextensive order with the private institution he is obliged to—namely, Mr. Knott's household.

Alain Badiou accordingly speaks of the poetic structure of Beckett's "ontological localization" as that of a "closure." He defines this as an arrangement of "a closed space, so that the set of features of the place of being may be enumerated and named with precision. The aim is that 'what is seen' be coextensive with 'what is said,' under the sign of the closed."[35] Badiou then suggests that Mr. Knott's house offers such a localization.[36] Here, the form of narration seeks the function of a closure and establishes an equation of focus and voice. With regard to the form of life, this means that the narrated form of life is in a somehow coextensive order with the institution of Mr. Knott's household. Other than in more traditional novels, we do not follow a form of life throughout its development, but find a form of life captured in a spatial order.

This leads to further consequences for the novel: as Beckett's novel constitutes such a closure, it not only ties the biographical form to an institution but it also replaces the proceeding temporal order by a spatial one: "For the new year says nothing new, to the man fixed in space."[37] The character's development is not a linear one, anymore (as that in traditional forms of novels) nor is the forming of his life. Instead, it is much more coextensive with the closed form of institution. This closure appears neither constricted nor is there anything missing:

> Watt had more and more the impression, as time passed, that nothing could be added to Mr. Knott's establishment, and from it nothing taken away, but that as it was now, so it had been in the beginning, and so it would remain to the end, in all essential respects, any significant presence, at any time, and here all presence was significant.[38]

It can be noted that the institution of Mr. Knott's household eliminates time ("as it was now, so it had been in the beginning, and so it would remain to the end") and seeks out one aim: its inner completion ("here all presence was significant"). It manages a form of self-organization and it stays implacable to any exception: any given thing from the outside must be carefully integrated,[39] and any withdrawal leads to mischief or confusion.[40] Without relying on any specific condition and seemingly just in a contingent manner, the institution of Mr. Knott produces an even more abstract and abstruse boundary of regimentation that is nevertheless strict. Such a procedure is known as the very ban of the law: an almost exact science with its own rules is set up hereby and it coordinates any eventuality of circumstances and thereby builds the dispositive of the novel.[41]

The narrated form of life is thus confronted with a form of order which in its various ways contradicts the novel's very own condition. Campe claimed that such a form of novel can be defined as the *novel of institution*, i.e., a literary genre mainly established in the first half of the twentieth century, realizing a different and complementary type of novel.[42] The novel of institution adopts, so the assumption, the form of the institution. And the institution is, in turn, revealed as a social form that is about to form life itself. Typically, these institutions would be the psychiatry, residential schools, or sanatoriums.[43] According to that, Beckett's novel can certainly be considered as a corresponding exemplar to this genre.[44] However, it is even more remarkable how the novel *Watt* is bound to the knot of a precise spatial order, which is not only that of the institution but that of a different type of literary genre that cannot be described as a mere novel. The poetic strategy of closure is in certain analogy with the novel of institution, but what is of more importance here: both share the spatial-narrative arrangement of an even more radical outbreak. The closure of *Watt* can then be understood as a closed and cosmic unity, which arises out of the tradition of the epic more than of a straight and developing plot typical of the modern novel.[45] Watt's perception thus describes Mr. Knott's house as a closed and complete cosmos that not only deals with mythical categories but also recalls Lukács's famous prescription of the epic:

> He feels it. The sensations, the premonitions of harmony are irrefragable, of immanent harmony, when all outside him will be he, the flowers the flowers that he is among him, the sky the sky that he is above him, the earth trodden the earth treading, and all sound his echo.[46]

While Claude Lévi-Strauss defines myth as a timeless entity,[47] Mr. Knott's house can certainly be seen as an estate of mythical time. The cosmos of Knott's establishment is bringing the plot close to a standstill and forces the novel's character into timeless domination.

("As it turned out, Watt was never to know how long he spent in Mr. Knott's house."[48]) So not only is Watt's mental health at stake, but the novel's very own conditions. The indifferent ontological levels of the myth and the eradication of a subject (as the novel's associated form of life) are a lethal threat to the self-given form of the novel. Once again, this shows the entanglement of the form of life and the form of the novel—and both are threatened by the mythical order of the epic. The law of Mr. Knott can thus be described as double-sided: on the one hand, it commands the forming of life of the novel's character and brings it in a closed and spatial order. On the other hand, the novel itself falls under the spell of an epic, total, and desubjectivizing narrative.[49]

The poetic strategy of *Watt* is, therefore, self-subtraction to the point of being a minimal difference: against an epic and cosmic unity, it insists on the autonomous negativity of the subject and on its forming of life. Beckett stays true to his poetics of a "worldlessness [Akosmismus] become flesh," as Adorno once claimed.[50] This leaves behind the tradition of the novel of institutions as well as that of the epic and brings the problem of form, life, and novel to the highest form of contradiction. The novel does so, however, by insisting on its innermost core—the death drive.

## The Novel's Death Drive

The novel's character Watt is presented as an arbitrary and sometimes even uncanny figure who finds an exquisite and deviant pleasure in short moments of destruction:

> Birds of every kind abounded, and these it was our delight to pursue, with stones and clods of earth. Robins, in particular, thanks to their confidingness, we destroyed in great numbers. And larks' nests, laden with eggs still warm from the mother's breast, we ground into fragments, under our feet, with peculiar satisfaction, at the appropriate time of the year.[51]

In solely pursuing his own task and want, with no regard to any given form (of life), he experiences this excess of lust even as divine: "It was on these occasions, we agreed, after an exchange of views, that we came nearest to God."[52] Watt's outbursts of lust show in typically *repetitive* behavior, as he incessantly scratches himself, picks his nose, snites, and gnashes his teeth.[53] But what is of interest for the novel's form of life is how this is realized *in* the novel's own syntax and form. So, while the theory of the novel is about the forming of life, the form of life that is found in the novel *Watt* instead persists as a rest that cannot be formed. There is a somehow inerasable rest persisting throughout the novel that continuously produces an inner unrest: an inner and impenetrable excess that generates incessant questions, abstruse sceneries,[54] long chains of possibilities,[55] and enduring performing of perpetual and seemingly endlessly repeating movements:

> To and fro, from the door to the window, from the window to the door; from the window to the door, from the door to the window; from the fire to the bed, from the bed to the fire; from the bed to the fire, from the fire to the bed; from the door to the fire, from the fire to the door; from the fire to the door, from the door to the fire; from the window to the bed, from the bed to the window; from

the bed to the window, from the window to the bed; from the fire to the window, from the window to the fire; from the window to the fire, from the fire to the window; from the bed to the door, from the door to the bed; from the door to the bed, from the bed to the door; from the door to the window, from […].[56]

It can thus be said that this strange ability to resist being formed, the emphatic insisting on "nothing," and the exalting production of grammatical deadlocks are the uttering of subjectivity at its very point of emergence. It is crucial to remark that all these iterations, permutations, and ongoing bad infinities that pervade the novel all mark firstly, a *symbolic* origin, and, secondly, they do this by *performing* it in the poetic structure. They are thus not just constituted on the level of the signifier, but they also realize this level itself throughout the novel. Not only does the novel describe the ongoing repetitions, compulsive acts, and intellectual obsessions, but it performs them itself. Just to give one example, consider the narrator's description of Mr. Knott:

> For one day Mr Knott would be tall, fat, pale and dark, and the next thin, small, flushed and fair, and the next sturdy, middlesized, yellow and ginger, and the next small, fat, pale and fair, and the next middlesized, flushed, thin and ginger, and the next tall, yellow, dark and sturdy, and the next fat, middlesized, ginger and pale, and the next tall, thin, dark and flushed, and the next small, fair, sturdy and yellow, and the next tall, ginger, pale and fat, and the next thin, flushed, small and dark, and the next fair, sturdy, middlesized and yellow, and the next dark, small, fat and pale, and

the next fair, middlesized, flushed and thin, and the next sturdy, ginger, tall and yellow, and the next [...].[57]

At first glance, these verbal anomalies might threaten the novel's understanding as a rational and vivid form. They might even present a thoughtless, juxtaposed, and uninspired excess of automatisms, an endless compulsion to repeat, mirroring the mental decline of the novel's character.[58] But this assumption falls short with regard to the form of the novel and its poetic strategy: the novel's insistence in a formless form is the very form of the novel, however, subtracted to its bones. Resisting any measure of forming, it preserves its very own negativity as a form of self-difference. The mode in which the form of life manages to maintain itself is that of insisting on the simplest and filthiest drives, the most neurotic forms of stubbornness, subjective idiosyncrasies, and the ongoing doubting of anything given.[59] The novel is thus not a mere reduction to inner drives, but rather to an inner connection between drive and signification—or in other words: the death drive.

The constant and programmatic *compulsion to repeat*, which is per definition a manifestation of the death drive, is thus a substantial part of the novel's poetics.[60] The iterations and variations get extended in the syntax of the novel, not just to produce and reproduce further irritation, but much more to maintain a very distinct poetic principle. Therefore, they might even be understood as an original poetic act of sublimation of the death drive, applied to the subjectivity that is at stake.[61] The novel itself reveals that it produces a difference in form and thereby differs from any other form—and this is precisely the opposing principle of life whereby subjectivity is defined. Even more, the novel can be understood as the precise ongoing performance of forming with which the act of subjectivation is being performed in a symbolic order. *Watt* is then the performing exhaustion of life into an individual story that marks the very sublimation of a subject's death drive.

Two points should be clarified at this step of the discussion: first, the poetic act of linking the drive to the symbolic function should not be mistaken with what Lacan calls "*lalangue*," referring to a deviant pleasure directed against all normative and reasonable aspects of language.[62] Beckett's poetic strategy is not about an illicit pleasure with words, but instead about the illicit point where words and subjectivity encounter each other. Secondly, it is of crucial importance to clarify the distinction between subject and subjectivity (as Jonathan Boulter also highlights in his reading of Beckett).[63] Following Boulter, Beckett's novels can be understood as a proceeding reduction of subjectivity, leaving behind bare subjects, understood as an undead rest or embodiment of an immortal drive.[64] As important as the distinction between subjectivity and subject for Beckett's poetics is, such an interpretation loses sight of the dialectics of both entities: by taking into account the crucial role of the death drive, it becomes clear that the novel's character Watt is not just reduced to an undead rest. Instead, this reduction uncovers the point where the drive is bound to language and where subjectivity is constituted.

With regard to the form of the novel *Watt*, it can now be claimed that its condition is not just at stake throughout the novel but that it resists against any heteronymous forming by insisting in the novel's specific own point of emergence: subjectivity. The death drive is thus an excess of life and an act of a minimal, but pure and free will:

> Then the gnashing ends, or it goes on, and one is in the pit, in the hollow, the longing for longing gone, the horror of horror, and one is in the hollow, at the foot of all the hills at last, the ways down, the ways up, and free, free at last, for an instant free at last, nothing at last.[65]

It is thus exactly its poetic structure with which the novel *Watt* cuts the umbilical cord to a heteronomous forming of life. Again, this not only displays a mere undead rest, but this rest is bound to the poetic structure and, therefore, to a will that is uttered in the form of the novel. A striking example for this is the attached "Addenda":[66] this alienated, extime part is a specific piece of afterbirth of the form of life of the novel. It is no living object ("never been born properly"),[67] nor form for itself or even simply poetic "waste." Still, it is bound to the novel and presents an inalienable part of it.

The novel finally shows a character Watt, who somehow manages to traverse the phantasm of a closed cosmos (understood as the service in the closure of Mr. Knott's house), just to maintain its minimal difference of subjectivity. Meanwhile, on the level of form, the novel manages to maintain a *subjective* form by traversing the phantasm of the epic. Watt's story is therefore told from the end, after the totality of the epic and with defining Watt's resisting form of life *as* being that of the novel: "As Watt told the beginning of his story, not first, but second, so not fourth, but third, now he told its end. Two, one, four, three, that was the order in which Watt told his story."[68] Watt insists on an arbitrary order, chooses different voices and foci, which just proves the very subjectivity of the novel. It is thus crucial that the novel is told from a retrospective view and as the story of the novel's character.[69] So, within the novel, its character Watt builds his unity as a subject beyond the temporal totality of the epic. It does so by bringing itself into a symbolic order, which is at the same time the poetic act of subjectivization: from Watt to *Watt*, so to speak.

All these images of destructive lust and deviant pleasure, the steadily repeated and slightly varied poetic formulas, the inerasable rests of language in the text, the wild permutations and the mentioned "Addenda" together have only one single and unsettling aim: they transport a death drive into the narrated form of life that is the novel. In the course of this process, the subject's negativity is uncovered as the poetic structure of the novel itself: "And if I could begin it all over again a hundred times, knowing each time a little more than before, the result would always be the same, and the hundredth life as the first, and hundred lives as one. A cat's flux."[70] The presented subjectivity opposes any process or development, let alone any poetological formula. But in the same sense, it is not a simple reduction to an undead, partial object. The novel *Watt* rejects both options and instead insists on subjectivity as the lowest but purest level of antagonism. The ongoing and tormenting question after "what forms life?" thus finds no answer in the novel apart from this restless, doubting, and incessantly questioning form of life that is *Watt*.

# Notes

1. The entanglement of the concepts "novel," "theory," and "life" has been a much-discussed topos in literature studies. See, for example, for this discussion Roland Barthes, *Writing Degree Zero*, trans. Annette Lavers and Colin Smith. (London: Jonathan Cape, 1967); Hans Blumenberg, "Wirklichkeitsbegriff und Möglichkeit des Romans," in *Ästhetische und metaphorologische Schriften*, ed. Anselm Haverkamp (Frankfurt am Main: Suhrkamp, 2001), 47–73; Rüdiger Campe, "Form and Life in the Theory of the Novel," *Constellations* 18, no. 1 (2011): 53–66; Franco Moretti, *The Way of the World: The Bildungsroman in European Culture* (London/New York: Verso, 2000); David Wellbery, "Die Enden des Menschen: Antropologie und Einbildungskraft im Bildungsroman (Wieland, Goethe, Novalis)," in *Das Ende: Poetik und Hermeneutik XVI*, ed. Karl Heinz Stierle (München: Fink, 1996), 600–39.

2. Cf. Campe, "Form and Life in the Theory of the Novel," 193–4; *Vita aesthetica. Szenarien ästhetischer Lebendigkeit*, ed. Armen Avanessian, Winfried Menninghaus, and Jan Völker (Zürich: Diaphanes, 2009), 15; Jan Völker, "Onto-Genesis der Form," in *Form: Zwischen Ästhetik und künstlerischer Praxis*, ed. Armen Avanessian, Franck Hofmann, Susanne Leeb, and Hans Stauffacher (Zürich: Diaphanes, 2009), 109–23.

3. Novalis, "Teplitzer Fragmente," in *Schriften: Die Werke Friedrich von Hardenbergs*, vol. II, ed. Paul Kluckhohn and Richard Samuel (Stuttgart: Kohlhammer, 1960–77), 559 [my translation]. For an English translation (although without the given quotation), cf. Novalis, *Philosophical Writings*, trans. and ed. Margaret Mahony Stoljar (New York: State University of New York Press, 1997), 101–10.

4. Campe, "Form and Life," 54.

5. Cf. Friedrich Schlegel, "Das Gespräch über die Poesie," in *Kritische Friedrich-Schlegel-Ausgabe*, vol. 2, ed. Ernst Behler et al. (München: Schöningh, 1958), 337. For the relation of organism and art cf. Claudia Blümle and Armin Schäfer, "Organismus und Kunstwerk. Zur Einführung," in *Struktur, Figur, Kontur: Abstraktion in Kunst und Lebenswissenschaft*, ed. Claudia Blümle and Armin Schäfer (Zürich: Diaphanes, 2007), 9–25; Leif Weatherby, *Transplanting the Metaphysical Organ: German Romanticism between Leibniz and Marx* (New York: Fordham, 2016).

6. The term "form of life" features prominently in the work of Agamben. Cf. Giorgio Agamben, *Homo Sacer: Sovereign Power and Bare Life* (Stanford, CA: Stanford University Press, 1998). According to Agamben, the term marks an ambivalence between juridical and biological semantics. For a discussion of this term, cf. Eva Geulen, "Form-of-Life/Forma-di-Vita:

Distinction in Agamben," in *Literatur als Philosophie*, ed. Bettine Menke and Eva Horn (München: Fink, 2006), 363–74.

7   Regarding the close relationship between subjectivity and the poetics of the novel, cf. Gerhart von Graevenitz, *Die Setzung des Subjekts: Untersuchungen zur Romantheorie* (Tübingen: Niemeyer, 1973); Peter Szondi, *Poetik und Geschichtsphilosophie* (Frankfurt am Main: Suhrkamp, 1974).

8   Cf. Étienne Balibar, "Subjection and Subjectivation," in *Supposing the Subject*, ed. Joan Copjec (London/New York: Verso, 1994), 1–16; René Descartes, *Meditations on First Philosophy*, trans. and ed. John Cottingham (Cambridge: Cambridge University Press, 1996).

9   Cf. Immanuel Kant, *Critique of Pure Reason*, trans. and ed. Paul Guyer and Allen W. Wood (Cambridge: Cambridge University Press, 1998), B 485, 508. Kant takes this step in the "Transcendental Dialectics" of his first *Critique*. The four antinomies correspond to the four classes of the table of categories. By identifying the categories of quantity, quality, modality, and relation, Kant suggests that the cosmos causes inevitable contradictions either in mathematical (i.e., in relation to its size) or in dynamical relations (i.e., with regard of the existence of its phenomena). Cf. Kant, *Critique of Pure Reason*, B 435-596, 460-550. For further discussions cf. Brigitte Falkenburg, *Kants Kosmologie: Die wissenschaftliche Revolution der Naturphilosophie im 18. Jahrhundert* (Frankfurt am Main: Suhrkamp, 2000); Slavoj Žižek, *The Ticklish Subject: The Absent Centre of Political Ontology* (London/New York: Verso, 1999), 59. In the "Addenda" of Beckett's novel *Watt*, one can find traces of Kant: "das fruchtbare Bathos der Erfahrung"—which is an allusion to Kant's *Prolegomena*. Samuel Beckett, *Watt*, ed. Chris J. Ackerley (London: Faber and Faber, 2009), 222.

10  Kant, *Critique of Pure Reason*, B 547 525.

11  Cf. Kant, *Critique of Pure Reason*, B 547 525, B 541, 522. The regulative idea of the world, however, still plays a crucial role in Kant's practical philosophy.

12  Georg Lukács, *The Theory of the Novel: A Historico-philosophical Essay on the Forms of Great Epic Literature*, trans. Anna Bostock (London: Merlin, 1971), 32. Regarding Lukács's philosophical development, cf. Andreas Hoeschen, *Das ‚Dostojewski'-Projekt': Lukács' neukantianisches Frühwerk in seinem ideengeschichtlichen Kontext* (München: Niemeyer, 1999).

13  Lukács, *Theory of the Novel*, 35.

14  Ibid., 16. For the relation of Beckett and Lukács cf. David Weisberg, *Chronicles of Disorder: Samuel Beckett and the Cultural Politics of the Modern Novel* (New York: State University of New York Press, 2000), 117.

15  Cf. Lukács: "But what is contained between the beginning and the end escapes the biographical categories of the process: it is the *eternally existent becoming* of ecstasy." Lukács, *Theory of the Novel*, 81.

16  Apart from Slavoj Žižek, whose work will be discussed below, also Mladen Dolar and Alenka Zupančičs try to philosophically establish the importance of the concept of the death drive. See Alenka Zupančič, *Ethics of the Real: Kant and Lacan* (London/New York: Verso, 2000).

17  Cf. Sigmund Freud, *Beyond the Pleasure Principle*, trans. and ed. James Strachey (London/New York: W. W. Norton & Co., 1961), 1–58.

18  Ibid., 32.

19  Ibid., 8, 26.

20  Lacan's "return to Freud" is explicitly motivated by his engagement with the concept of the death drive, cf. Jacques Lacan, *The Seminar, Book II, the Ego in Freud's Theory and in the Technique of Psychoanalysis, 1954–1955*, ed. Jacques-Alain Miller, trans. Sylvana Tomaselli (London/New York: W. W. Norton & Co., 1988); Jacques Lacan, *The Seminar, Book VII, the Ethics of Psychoanalysis, 1959–1960*, ed. Jacques-Alain Miller, trans. Dennis Porter (London/ New York: W. W. Norton & Co., 1992).

21  Lacan, *The Ethics of Psychoanalysis*, 211.

22  Jacques Lacan, *Écrits*, trans. Bruce Fink (London/New York: W. W. Norton & Co., 2002), 848.

23  Žižek defines the death drive as "the empty frame within which the game of historization is taking place." Slavoj Žižek, "The Abyss of Freedom," in *The Abyss of Freedom. Ages of the World*, ed. Friedrich Wilhelm Joseph von Schelling and Slavoj Žižek (Ann Arbor: University of Michigan Press, 1997), 38.

24  Žižek, *The Ticklish Subject*, 50.

25  Žižek, *Abyss of Freedom*, 43.

26  Žižek, *Ticklish Subject*, 36.

27  Peter Brooks first highlighted the structural parallels between the death drive and the inner drive of the narrative as a whole. Cf. Peter Brooks, *Reading for the Plot: Design and Intention in Narrative* (Cambridge, MA/ London: Harvard University Press, 1984), 320. While Brooks focuses on the relevance of psychoanalysis and the narrative for the plot, he misses some crucial aspects regarding subjectivity and the novel. It can be noted that there is a strong connection between the death drive, narration, and the subject.

28  I will not go into detail regarding the later work of Beckett. It can be claimed, however, that he discusses these aspects again in detail in his *Texts for Nothing*, Cf. Samuel Beckett, *Texts for Nothing and Other Shorter Prose, 1950–1976*, ed. Mark Nixon (London: Faber and Faber, 2010).

29  For the historic and biographic circumstances of the genesis of the novel cf. Chris J. Ackerley, *Obscure Locks, Simple Keys: The Annotated "Watt"* (Edinburgh: Edinburgh University Press, 2010); Andrew Gibson, "French Beckett and French Literary Politics 1945–52," in *The Edinburgh Companion to Samuel Beckett and the Arts*, ed. Stanley E. Gontarski (Edinburgh: Edinburgh University Press, 2014), 103–16.

30  Mark Nixon understands Watt's "fragmentary structure" and "inconclusiveness" as a result of the clear influence of Beckett's diary writings. Cf. Mark Nixon, *Samuel Beckett's German Diaries 1936–1937* (London/New York: Continuum, 2011), 33.

31  A quite controversial discussion can be found in Giorgio Agamben, *Remnants of Auschwitz: The Witness and the Archive* (New York: Zone Books, 1999), 69.

32  However, one can notice a shift in the discussion toward a more sociological reading of this complex relation. This shift is already present in Lukács's *Theory of the Novel* (and in his planned book on Dostoevsky). Furthermore, I will not go into detail regarding the "vitalistic" aspect of Beckett's poetics, which might lead to Bergson and Deleuze. For such an interpretation, cf. Gilles Deleuze, *Bergsonism* (New York: Zone Books, 1988); Stanley E. Gontarski, "Recovering Beckett's Bergsonism," in *Beckett at 100: Revolving It All*, ed. Linda Ben-Zvi and Angela Moorjani (Oxford: Oxford University Press, 2008), 93–106.

33  In this regard, Goethe seems to be of great importance for Beckett, as the latter provides long transcriptions from Goethe's *Dichtung und Wahrheit*. Cf. Nixon, *Beckett's German Diaries*, 67. One reason for this might be the strong connection between life and form that Goethe's work is famous for. It can be said that Beckett sticks to this tradition until his first trilogy.

34  Beckett, *Watt*, 62.

35  Alain Badiou, *On Beckett*, ed. Nina Power and Alberto Toscano (London: Clinamen Press, 2003), 5.

36  Cf. ibid.

37  Beckett, *Watt*, 113.

38  Ibid., 112.

39  For example, the visit of Mr. Gall and his son reveals a "fugitive penetrating" when they tune the well-tempered piano and thereby disturb the inner cosmic harmony of the household. Ibid., 57.

40  For example, the food withdrawals are given to a dog in a strict and complex regalement. Ibid., 73.

41  "For he knew, as though he had been told, that the receipt of this dish had never varied, since its establishment, long long before, and that the choice, the dosage and the quantities of the elements employed had been calculated, with the most minute exactness, to afford Mr. Knott, in a course of fourteen full meals, that is to say, seven full luncheons, and seven full dinners, the maximum of pleasure compatible with the protraction of his health." Ibid., 73. For the concept of the ban of the law cf. Eric Santner, *On the Psychotheology of Everyday Life* (Chicago, IL: University of Chicago Press, 2007), 62.

42  Cf. Rüdiger Campe, "Robert Walsers Institutionenroman. Jakob von Gunten," in *Die Macht und das Imaginäre: Eine kulturelle Verwandtschaft in der Literatur zwischen Früher Neuzeit und Moderne*, ed. Roger Behrens and Jörn Steigerwald (Würzburg: Königshausen & Neumann, 2005), 238; Rüdiger Campe, "Kafkas Institutionenroman: *Der Proceß, Das Schloß*," in *Gesetz, Ironie, Festschrift für Manfred Schneider*, ed. Rüdiger Campe and Michael Niehaus (Heidelberg: Synchron, 2004), 197–208.

43  Campe sees the early modern and baroque novel as the starting point for this tradition. He further clarifies that this tradition is a specific genre (this might not be by chance) of the German landscape. Kafka's famous novels *The Trial* and *The Castle*, Robert Walser's early writings, as well as Thomas Mann's *The Magic Mountain*, among others, can be called typical examples of the novel of institution in the early twentieth century.

44  Watt himself speaks of Mr. Knott's establishment and their rules as of a "venerable tradition, or institution." Beckett, *Watt*, 98.

45  Cf. Badiou: "It could therefore be believed that we are here in the midst of typically predestined universe. Knowledge lacks any kind of freedom; it consists of questions relative to the laws of the place. It is a question of attempting, forever in vain, to understand the impenetrable designs of Mr. Knott." Badiou, *On Beckett*, 56.

46  Lukács, *Theory of the Novel*, 33. Cf. the famous passage of Lukács: "Happy are those ages when the starry sky is the map of all possible paths—ages whose paths are illuminated by the light of the stars. Everything in such ages is new and yet familiar, full of adventure and yet their own. The world is wide and yet it is like a home, for the fire that burns in the soul is of the same essential nature as the stars; the world and the self, the light and the fire, are sharply distinct, yet they never become permanent strangers to one another, for fire is the soul of all light and all fire clothes itself in light." Ibid., 28. Lukács's later readings of Beckett will not be part of our discussion here. For this cf. Georg Lukács, *The Meaning of Contemporary Realism* (London: Merlin Press, 1963).

47  Cf. Claude Lévi-Strauss, *Structural Anthropology*, trans. Claire Jacobson and Brooke Grundfest Schoepf (New York: Basic Books, 1963), 209.

48  Beckett, *Watt*, 116.

49  Put differently: the epic is already some modus of subjective narration, and the subjective narrative reverts to the epic—to once more modify Adorno's and Horkheimer's phrase. Cf. Theodor W. Adorno and Max Horkheimer, *Dialectic of Enlightenment: Philosophical Fragments* (Stanford, CA: Stanford University Press, 2002), xviii.

50  Cf. Theodor W. Adorno. "Trying to Understand *Endgame*," in *Notes to Literature*, vol. 1, ed. Rolf Tiedemann, trans. Shierry Weber Nicholsen (New York: Columbia University Press, 1991), 251. The novel's character Watt explicitly utters his acosmism: "For if there were two things that Watt disliked, one was the moon and the other was the sun." Beckett, *Watt*, 27. Or in brief: "And the poor old lousy old earth, my earth and my father's and my mother's and my father's father's and my mother's mother's […]. An excrement." Ibid., 38.

51  Ibid., 132.

52  Ibid.

53  See for these aspects of subjectivity in Beckett, Armin Schäfer, "Erschöpfte Literatur. Über das Neue bei Samuel Beckett," in *Null, Nichts und Negation: Beckett's No-thing*, ed. Karin Kröger and Armin Schäfer (Bielefeld: transcript, 2016), 234. Regarding the repetitive poetics of *Watt*, cf. Steven Connor. *Samuel Beckett: Repetition, Theory and Text* (Aurora: The Davies Group, 2006), 17. For the aspects of "liberty" of such compulsions cf. Slavoj Žižek, *Enjoy Your Symptom! Jacques Lacan in Hollywood and Out* (London: Routledge, 1992), 69.

54  Cf. Beckett, *Watt*, 78.

55  E.g.: "Twelve possibilities occurred to Watt, in this connection […]." Ibid., 74. Watt even designs lists with different solutions, "but also some of those objections that were perhaps the cause of their not having done so." Ibid., 81.

56  Ibid., 176.

57  Ibid., 181.

58  Cf. the kind of private language Watt develops in the later part of the novel. Ibid., 303.

59  When Badiou speaks of the Cartesian *cogito* regarding Beckett's poetics, he indicates a distinctive potential: "On the one hand, an excess so violent that it destroys not language but the subject and, on the other, a lack which in vain exposes the subject to the throes of 'dying', places the subject of the Beckettian Cogito in a state of genuine terror." Badiou, *On Beckett*, 52. For the relation to Descartes cf. Steven Connor, *Samuel Beckett*; Samuel Mintz, "Beckett's Murphy: A 'Cartesian Novel,'" *Perspective* 2, no. 3 (1959): 156–65;

and Samuel Beckett, "Whoroscope," in *Collected Poems*, ed. Séan Lawlor and John Pilling (London: Faber and Faber, 2013), 40–3.

60  Jonathan Boulter (among others) already highlighted this point. See Jonathan Boulter, *Beckett: A Guide for the Perplexed* (London/New York: Bloomsbury, 2008), 92–4; Daniel Katz, *Saying I No More: Subjectivity and Consciousness in the Prose of Samuel Beckett* (Evanston: Northwestern University Press, 1999), 142; Thomas Trezise, *Into the Breach: Samuel Beckett and the Ends of Literature* (Princeton, NJ: Princeton University Press, 1990), 91.

61  Sublimation in this sense does not mean a dissolution in "higher" cultural forms but refers to a connection between the drive and the symbolic function, cf. Lacan, *The Seminar, Book VII, the Ethics of Psychoanalysis*, 205–17.

62  Cf. Jacques Lacan, *The Seminar, Book XX, Encore: On Feminine Sexuality, the Limits of Love and Knowledge, 1972–1973*, ed. Jacques-Alain Miller, trans. Bruce Fink (London/New York: W. W. Norton & Co., 1998), 126.

63  Boulter refers to Blanchot's remark on "subjectivity without a subject"—one part just reveals itself by reducing the other. Cf. Boulter, *Beckett: A Guide for the Perplexed*, 83.

64  Ibid.

65  Beckett, *Watt*, 174.

66  Ibid., 215.

67  Ibid., 217.

68  Ibid., 186.

69  This does not touch the question of who might be the narrator of the novel. For this complex, cf. for example. Trezise, *Into the Breach*, 6.

70  Beckett, *Watt*, 39.

# Bibliography

Ackerley, Chris. *Obscure Locks, Simple Keys: The Annotated "Watt."* Edinburgh: Edinburgh University Press, 2010.

Adorno, Theodor W. "Trying to Understand *Endgame*." In *Notes to Literature*, vol. 1, edited by Rolf Tiedemann, translated by Shierry Weber Nicholsen, 241–75. New York: Columbia University Press, 1991.

Adorno, Theodor W. and Max Horkheimer. *Dialectic of Enlightenment: Philosophical Fragments*. Stanford, CA: Stanford University Press, 2002.

Agamben, Giorgio. *Homo Sacer: Sovereign Power and Bare Life*. Stanford, CA: Stanford University Press, 1998.

Agamben, Giorgio. *Remnants of Auschwitz: The Witness and the Archive*. New York: Zone Books, 1999.

Avanessian, Armen, Winfried Menninghaus, and Jan Völker, ed. *Vita aesthetica. Szenarien ästhetischer Lebendigkeit*. Zürich: Diaphanes, 2009.

Badiou, Alain. *On Beckett*, edited by Nina Power and Alberto Toscano. London: Clinamen Press, 2003.

Balibar, Étienne. "Subjection and Subjectivation." In *Supposing the Subject*, edited by Joan Copjec, 1–16. London/New York: Verso, 1994.

Barthes, Roland. *Writing Degree Zero*, translated by Annette Lavers and Colin Smith. London: Jonathan Cape, 1967.

Beckett, Samuel. *Watt*, edited by Chris J. Ackerley. London: Faber and Faber, 2009.

Beckett, Samuel. *Texts for Nothing and Other Shorter Prose. 1950–1976*, edited by Mark Nixon. London: Faber and Faber, 2010.

Blumenberg, Hans. "Wirklichkeitsbegriff und Möglichkeit des Romans." In *Ästhetische und metaphorologische Schriften*, edited by Anselm Haverkamp, 47–73. Frankfurt am Main: Suhrkamp, 2001.

Blümle, Claudia and Armin Schäfer. "Organismus und Kunstwerk. Zur Einführung." In *Struktur, Figur, Kontur: Abstraktion in Kunst und Lebenswissenschaft*, edited by Claudia Blümle and Armin Schäfer, 9–25. Zürich: Diaphanes, 2007.

Boulter, Jonathan. *Beckett: A Guide for the Perplexed*. London/New York: Bloomsbury, 2008.

Brooks, Peter. *Reading the Plot: Design and Intention in Narrative*. Cambridge, MA/London: Harvard University Press, 1984.

Campe, Rüdiger. "Form and Life in the Theory of the Novel." *Constellations* 18, no. 1 (2011): 53–66.

Campe, Rüdiger. "Robert Walsers Institutionenroman. Jakob von Gunten." In *Die Macht und das Imaginäre: Eine kulturelle Verwandtschaft in der Literatur zwischen Früher Neuzeit und Moderne*, edited by Roger Behrens and Jörn Steigerwald, 235–50. Würzburg: Königshausen & Neumann, 2005.

Campe, Rüdiger. "Kafkas Institutionenroman: Der Proceß, Das Schloß." In *Gesetz, Ironie, Festschrift für Manfred Schneider*, edited by Rüdiger Campe and Michael Niehaus, 197–208. Heidelberg: Synchron, 2004.

Deleuze, Gilles. *Bergsonism*. New York: Zone Books, 1988.

Descartes, René. *Meditations on First Philosophy*, translated and edited by John Cottingham. Cambridge: Cambridge University Press, 1996.

Falkenburg, Brigitte. *Kants Kosmologie: Die wissenschaftliche Revolution der Naturphilosophie im 18. Jahrhundert*. Frankfurt am Main: Suhrkamp, 2000.

Freud, Sigmund. *Beyond the Pleasure Principle*, translated and edited by James Strachey. London/New York: W. W. Norton & Co., 1961.

Geulen, Eva. "Form-of-Life / Forma-di-Vita: Distinction in Agamben." In *Literatur als Philosophie*, edited by Bettine Menke and Eva Horn, 363–74. München: Fink, 2006.
Gibson, Andrew. "French Beckett and French Literary Politics 1945–1952." In *The Edinburgh Companion to Samuel Beckett and the Arts*, edited by Stanley E. Gontarski, 103–16. Edinburgh University Press, 2014.
Gontarski, Stanley E. "Recovering Beckett's Bergsonism." In *Beckett at 100. Revolving It All*, edited by Linda Ben-Zvi and Angela Moorjani, 93–106. Oxford: Oxford University Press, 2008.
Graevenitz, Gerhart von. *Die Setzung des Subjekts: Untersuchungen zur Romantheorie*. Tübingen: Niemeyer, 1973.
Hoeschen, Andreas. *Das "Dostojewski‹-Projekt": Lukács' neukantianisches Frühwerk in seinem ideengeschichtlichen Kontext*. München: Niemeyer, 1999.
Kant, Immanuel. *Critique of Pure Reason*, translated and edited by Paul Guyer and Allen W. Wood. Cambridge: Cambridge University Press, 1998.
Lacan, Jacques. *The Seminar. Book II. The Ego in Freud's Theory and in the Technique of Psychoanalysis. 1954–1955*, edited by Jacques-Alain Miller, translated by Sylvana Tomaselli. London/New York: W. W. Norton & Co., 1961.
Lacan, Jacques. *The Seminar. Book VII. The Ethics of Psychoanalysis. 1959–1960*, edited by Jacques-Alain Miller, translated by Dennis Porter. London/New York: W. W. Norton & Co., 1992.
Lacan, Jacques. *Écrits*, translated by Bruce Fink. London/New York: W. W. Norton & Co., 2002.
Lévi-Strauss, Claude. *Structural Anthropology*, translated by Claire Jacobson and Brooke Grundfest Schoepf. New York: Basic Books, 1963.
Lukács, Georg. *The Meaning of Contemporary Realism*. London: Merlin Press, 1963.
Lukács, Georg. *The Theory of the Novel: A Historico-philosophical Essay on the Forms of Great Epic Literature*, translated by Anna Bostock. London: Merlin, 1971.
Moretti, Franco. *The Way of the World: The Bildungsroman in European Culture*. London/New York: Verso, 2000.
Nixon, Mark. *Samuel Beckett's German Diaries 1936–1937*. London/New York: Continuum, 2011.
Novalis. "Teplitzer Fragmente." In *Schriften. Die Werke Friedrich von Hardenbergs*, vol. 2, edited by Paul Kluckhohn and Richard Samuel, 595–622. Stuttgart: Kohlhammer, 1960–77.
Novalis. *Philosophical Writings*, translated by Margaret Mahony Stoljar. New York: State University of New York Press, 1997.
Santner, Eric. *On the Psychotheology of Everyday Life*. Chicago, IL: University of Chicago Press, 2007.
Schäfer, Armin. "Erschöpfte Literatur. Über das Neue bei Samuel Beckett." In *Null, Nichts und Negation: Beckett's No-thing*, edited by Karin Kröger and Armin Schäfer, 225–45. Bielefeld: transcript, 2016.

Schlegel, Friedrich. "Das Gespräch über die Poesie." In *Kritische Friedrich-Schlegel-Ausgabe*, vol. 2, edited by Ernst Behler et al., 284–351. München: Schöningh, 1958.

Szondi, Peter. *Poetik und Geschichtsphilosophie*. Frankfurt am Main: Suhrkamp, 1974, 2974.

Völker, Jan. "Onto-Genesis der Form." In *Form: Zwischen Ästhetik und künstlerischer Praxis*, edited by Armen Avanessian, Franck Hofmann, Susanne Leeb, and Hans Stauffacher, 109–23. Zürich: Diaphanes, 2009.

Weatherby, Leif. *Transplanting the Metaphysical Organ: German Romanticism between Leibniz and Marx*. New York: Fordham, 2016.

Weisberg, David. *Chronicles of Disorder: Samuel Beckett and the Cultural Politics of the Modern Novel*. New York: State University of New York Press, 2000.

Wellbery, David. "Die Enden des Menschen. Anthropologie und Einbildungskraft im Bildungsroman (Wieland, Goethe, Novalis)." In *Das Ende: Poetik und Hermeneutik XVI*, edited by Karl Heinz Stierle, 600–39. München: Fink, 1996.

Žižek, Slavoj. *Enjoy Your Symptom! Jacques Lacan in Hollywood and Out*. London: Routledge, 1992.

Žižek, Slavoj. "The Abyss of Freedom." In *The Abyss of Freedom. Ages of the World*, edited by Friedrich Wilhelm Joseph von Schelling and Slavoj Žižek, 3–104. Ann Arbor: University of Michigan Press, 1997.

Žižek, Slavoj. *The Ticklish Subject. The Absent Centre of Political Ontology*. London/New York: Verso, 1999.

Zupančič, Alenka. *Ethics of the Real: Kant and Lacan*. London/New York: Verso, 2000.

# VII

# No Louder: Beckett and the Dynamics of Monotony

Tadej Troha

If we attempt to concisely identify the difference between Beckett's earlier and late dramatic texts, we could encapsulate it in the difference between two short stage directions that appear in two clearly similar lines, the first taken from *Endgame* and the second from *Footfalls*:

> Forgive me. [*Pause. Louder.*] I said forgive me.[1]
>
> Forgive me again. [*Pause. No louder.*] Forgive me again.[2]

What do we imply by positing the difference between Beckett's first and second stage of playwriting as the difference between two stage directions, the one demanding the repetition of the line to be spoken out *louder* and the one demanding the repetition to be a strict repetition that should appear *no louder* than the first line? Simply that the early Beckett wagers on the intensity of the characters and the second on their faintness? Does the difference lie in his early playwriting still opening a space for some kind of psychological dynamics, while in the late Beckett, there remains nothing but a melancholy stasis, the staging of monotony without any dynamics?

Beckett's early playwriting already takes place in a space without a real echo, and one could hardly argue the sporadic changes in volume are to be taken as one of its fundamental features. Nevertheless, we can still find in it the dynamics in which speaking "louder" obtains a certain effect, albeit the sudden crescendo manifests not so much power as impotence (think only of Pozzo, whose grotesque theatricality stages, as it were, the impotent reaction of the dramatic tradition faced with a newly formed Beckettian universe).

Something of this sort, however, is no longer conceivable in late Beckett. His later figures can display extreme intensity; at times, they even literally act "louder" than the moments before: but even when they scream, the intensity is by no means an operator of inter-subjective power relations. Screaming in *Not I*, for example, a fascinating piece in which a mouth as a partial object appears on stage, is possible merely as a manifestation of pure intensity in an a-dialogical space, a space in which there is no room for the other (of the) Other:

> couldn't make the sound ... not any sound ... no sound of any kind ... no screaming for help for example ... should she feel so inclined ... scream ... [Screams.] ... then listen ... [Silence.] ... scream again ... [Screams again.] ... then listen again ... [Silence.] ... no ... spared that ... all silent as the grave ... no part– ... what? ... the buzzing? ... yes ... all silent but for the buzzing ... so-called ... no part of her moving ... that she could feel ...[3]

When we recognize that both a scream and a silence are ultimately only two manifestations of the intensity of an impersonal buzzing, we might provisionally conclude that in the louder/no louder pair the second stage direction appears as the truth of the first, i.e., not only as a recognition of the impotence of speaking louder but as a *recognized impotence*, the affirmation of the impossibility of even attempting to produce an effect by increasing the intensity.

In this sense, the final stage of Beckett's playwriting would make up for the lag behind his own prose, and catch up to the coordinates he laid out with the *Trilogy* precisely in the years when he staged *Waiting for Godot*, the coordinates of dissolving all differences into one single plane—coordinates correctly registered by pure listening, whose actual subject, as Beckett's Malone would have it, is not a human being but their ears, the ears of a psychical *apparatus*:

> But our business at the moment is less with these futilities than with my ears [...]. I note then, without emotion, that of late *their hearing* seems to have improved. Oh not that I was ever even incompletely deaf. But for a long time now I have been hearing things confusedly. There I go again. What I mean is possibly this, that the noises of the world, so various in themselves and which I used to be so clever at distinguishing from one another, had been dinning at me for so long, always the same old noises, as gradually to have merged into a single noise, so that all I heard was one vast continuous buzzing. The volume of sound perceived remained no doubt the same, I had simply lost the faculty of decomposing it. *The noises of nature, of mankind and even my own, were all jumbled*

*together in one and the same unbridled gibberish.* Enough. I would willingly attribute part of my shall I say my misfortunes to this disordered sense were I not unfortunately rather inclined to look upon it as a blessing. Misfortunes, blessings, I have no time to pick my words, I am in a hurry to be done.[4]

While in *Waiting for Godot* and *Endgame* the distinction between the characters is eliminated only secondarily, i.e., through reception and interpretation (Vladimir and Estragon are two, and yet they might be only two sides of one and the same character; Hamm and Clov are two, and yet it might all be merely a depiction of Hamm's inner state, with Clov being only a figment of his imagination), in late Beckett, classic inter-subjectivity disappears already at the diegetic level. Instead of inter-subjectivity, we have pure monologue (*A Piece of Monologue*), an individual's internal split into a figure and a voice (*Rockaby*), and a duplication of one character (*Ohio Impromptu*) into a reader and a listener "as alike in appearance as possible,"[5] or—on the other hand—different forms of pure collectives (the collective of speechless movers in *Quad*, the collective of three voices of the same person in *That Time*). Indeed, if we observe Beckett's development from this perspective, it is precisely the difference between "louder" and "no louder" that could effectively illustrate this shift—the shift from a world where "louder" no longer has any effect, to a world where speaking louder becomes strictly impossible.

However, the difference between "louder" and "no louder" becomes more than an apt illustration only under the condition that we understand stage directions as such in their primary function—

not as additional information assisting us in our reading of a dramatic text, but as instructions for the stage production. It is in this function that through the years they gradually acquired a practically ethical status for Beckett—insofar as they address the responsibility of the performers to resist spontaneous re-naturalization, spontaneous inventions within the given and declaratively accepted framework of a faithful staging, a staging to the letter. Put differently, stage directions are a test of whether Beckett's universe has been understood as a particular universe within the general universe or rather as the actual concretization of the latter, thus as a universe in which the ordinary criteria of what it is to make sense, to be effective on stage, to be performable and—last but not least—to be "Beckettian" are suspended.

To illustrate, in a somewhat banal fashion, how easily even the most well-intentioned staging can slip up, let us take an example from the first part of *Footfalls*, in which a dialogue between May (M) and the off-stage voice of her dead/undead mother, takes place on stage.

> M: Straighten your pillows? [*Pause.*] Change your drawsheet? [*Pause.*] Pass you the bedpan? [*Pause.*] The warming-pan? [*Pause.*] Dress your sores? [*Pause.*] Sponge you down? [*Pause.*] Moisten your poor lips? [*Pause.*] Pray with you? [*Pause.*] For you? [*Pause.*] Again.[6]

Here, the stage directions do not demand any particular effort, all they expect of the actor is to insert pauses persistently—and yet there can hardly be any doubt that an actor burdened by involuntary naturalism will find absolute fidelity to the text insufferable. An actor faced with these lines will obviously understand that the pauses are an indication of the text not being an entirely ordinary dialogue and will, therefore, accept that the pauses should, in principle, be adhered to. But if the actor and the director give in to the temptation to be inventive, they will introduce a completely different dynamics into the utterance of the lines.

Most pauses between the sentences will remain; some will disappear, while others will—as compensation—become longer, which is supposed to create precisely the unwritten atmosphere that Beckett is wagering on in the text. The actor will maintain the first few pauses, but then she will come to feel that it would be better to leave some out, to speed things up—just to open the space for a few substantial, long, dramatic pauses, the type of pauses that commonsensically befit the enraptured atmosphere of talking to one's dead/undead mother. Put differently, it is highly likely that the final result will be precisely as if there were no stage directions in the text—and the lines will ultimately be uttered thusly: "Straighten your pillows? [*Pause.*] Change your drawsheet? [*Pause.*] Pass you the bedpan? [*Short pause.*] The warming-pan? [*Long pause.*] Dress your sores? Sponge you down? Moisten your poor lips? [*Long pause.*] Pray with you? [*Long pause.*] For you? [*Pause.*] Again."

What such a stage translation—as I have already suggested above—shows, is not only an ambition to surpass Beckett's judgment of the general psychology of the character; when the actor introduces her own dynamics into the text, she will also be convinced that she outperforms Beckett in understanding his own theatrical universe.

She will forget that such a judgment is possible only on the basis of wholly internal criteria, criteria where the usual framework disappears, criteria where the elements give rise to internal relations that in the end prove to be quite logical although we would never have thought of them.

In the beginning, we proposed the hypothesis that two seemingly dispensable stage directions, *louder* and *no louder*, encapsulate the difference between the earlier and the late Beckett. In their original context, both of them direct the staging of the repetition of the same sentence. Schematically the difference is thus the following: x [*louder*] x // x [*no louder*] x.

The first formula of repetition, x [*louder*] x, is taken from *Endgame*:

HAMM: [*Shocked.*] I haven't made you suffer too much?
CLOV: Yes!
HAMM: [*Relieved.*] Ah you gave me a fright! [*Pause. Coldly.*] Forgive me. [*Pause. Louder.*] I said, Forgive me.
CLOV: I heard you.

And, again, just a few lines further:

CLOV: You shouldn't speak to me like that.
[*Pause*].
HAMM: [*Coldly.*] Forgive me. [*Pause. Louder.*] I said, Forgive me.
CLOV: I heard you.[7]

At first sight, the stage direction "louder" seems to be completely redundant. Just like in a real-life situation, we will scarcely find an actor on stage who would not spontaneously utter the second "forgive me" louder. Moreover, the redundancy seems to be all the more obvious due to the fact that what we are dealing with is not a pure repetition but a repetition with an addition, whereby the "I said" itself already implies some kind of gradation.

Yet, if we consider the broader context, namely, the abundance of the surrounding stage directions ("*shocked*," "*relieved*," "*coldly*,"), this stage direction becomes necessary in order for Beckett to maintain a minimal structural order. The frenetic mood swings are part of the character, and the character is, as such, part of the structure of the action on stage; it is therefore of fundamental importance to preclude any chance of the actor improvising on the material. The central message of the play is built up elsewhere; concretely, when it comes to this line and its micro-context, what matters is that it is repeated after a few pages, now being reduced to its minimum, transformed into its "no louder" version: (x [*louder*] x)—[*no louder*]—(x [*louder*] x)

It is important to note that it is on this level that the dynamics of the play, the direction toward "no-louderness," is given. And perhaps this also explains why the earlier Beckett plays are, at least to a certain extent, still immune to acting slips. It is the structure of the dramatic text itself that dictates its own staging. No matter how badly it is staged, it somehow still remains a Beckett play.

This is by no means true of the plays of late Beckett, which from the very outset operate in the field of *no louder*, i.e., in the field where to speak louder is not merely ineffective but strictly impossible. While we can still imagine an imperfect, but nevertheless solid staging of

*Godot* or *Endgame*, it is only in late Beckett that an imperfect staging proves to be fatal. Insofar as the texts themselves are conditioned by the faith in a perfect staging, the staging of plays such as *Footfalls*, *Not I*, or *Rockaby* can only be perfect, again perfect—or they cease to exist. The belief in the possibility of a perfect staging emerges as the condition of the structure of the text itself. The crucial thing here is not that the text, after it has been written, can be staged only in one correct way, but that this is what enables Beckett to start writing in the first place.

So what does the stage direction *no louder* designate in the concrete case, in *Footfalls*? When it appears between two identical sentences, it is—contrary to *louder*—counterintuitive in its very principle and never quite redundant: "Mother. [*Pause. No louder.*] Mother. / And I? [*Pause. No louder.*] And I? / Forgive me again. [*Pause. No louder.*] Forgive me again. / May. [*Pause. No louder.*] May."[8]

An actor faced with such repetitions will read the general guidance in the introductory note (both voices "low and slow throughout"),[9] but she will have difficulty resisting the temptation to emphasize the second sentence in some way or another. And if anything, the stage directions *no louder* says no more nor less than this: *be careful what you are doing*. Its key function is to draw attention to the fragility of the text, which is threatened with complete disintegration by the smallest slip in its performance, its stage realization.

And, yet, does this already mean that if we only follow the directions, *Footfalls* can be performed automatically, without any thought and without any concept? Certainly not. If, on the one hand, the "no louder" that appears within the text only affirms the general guidance, it, on the other hand, gives us the opportunity to search for the dynamics in something *less*, in the stage directions reduced to the meremost minimum: to the terrain of the pause.

Beckett created *Footfalls* based on two points of departure. The introductory note already makes it clear that what Beckett centers the play around is a quite simple—but for that very reason—much more precise choreography, the repetitive pacing of the only figure along the stage.

> MAY (M), *dishevelled grey hair, worn grey wrap hiding feet, trailing.*
> WOMAN'S VOICE (V) *from dark upstage.*
> *Strip: downstage, parallel with front, length nine steps, width one metre, a little off centre audience right.*
>
> | L | r | l | r | l | r | L | r | l | R | ← | R |
> |---|---|---|---|---|---|---|---|---|---|---|---|
> | → | l | r | l | r | L | r | l | R | l |   |   |
>
> *Pacing: starting with right foot (r), from right (R) to left (L), with left foot (l) from L to R.*
> *Turn: rightabout at L, leftabout at R.*
> *Steps: clearly audible rhythmic tread.*[10]

As one can read in the rehearsal notes by Walter Asmus, who assisted Beckett in the 1976 Berlin production of the play, the acknowledgment of the central role of this stage action is also the precondition for the interpretation, both by the actor and of the meaning:

H[ildegard Schmall] says she has difficulties with the text. "I don't understand the play." Beckett emphasizes the importance of the footsteps. The walking up and down is the central image, he says. This was his basic conception of the play. The text, the words were only built up around this picture.[11]

The staging must if we explicate what is implied here, follow in full the order in which the play had been conceived. Just as Beckett conceived the play proceeding from the image and the sound of the steps, May must first perform this impression; she must find a way to stage the mere-steps.

Insofar as we are dealing with a performance of a ritual that cannot entirely suture the hole from which it is generated, the real content of *Footfalls* is precisely that which is generated beyond, but only through the steps. And in his conception of the character, Beckett had a particular figure in mind.

"But how is the figure of May to be understood then?"

Only hesitantly does Beckett take up this challenge to give more detailed information about the play. In the thirties, he says, C.G. Jung, the psychologist, once gave a lecture in London and told of a female patient who was being treated by him. Jung said he wasn't able to help this patient and for this, according to Beckett, he gave an astonishing explanation. *This girl wasn't living. She existed but didn't actually live.* According to Beckett, this story had impressed him very much at the time.[12]

Two elements were actually involved in the conception of the play; on the one hand, the story of Jung's patient, or better yet, a fragment of this story that—by being appropriated by Beckett—transcended the story itself; and, on the other, the image/sound of steps, which had appeared in his writing before, but merely as an auxiliary motif.

It is obvious that in *Footfalls*, Beckett managed to synthesize two fragments of the real which he found fascinating, and yet was not able to find a way to adequately "abreact" them. Two elements were involved, but it is crucial that the synthesis was possible only under the primacy of one of them, the fragment that had already figured in the phenomenal world, thus footsteps as the material moment on the basis of which the other fragment of the real can be generated in the concrete.

In light of this, it comes as no surprise that in his own production Beckett defined the steps even more precisely than in the original stage direction; but let there be no mistake, this is by no means a negation of the introductory note, but rather an explication of how we are to understand it if we do not wish to interpret it freely.

> The formal technical course of the play is made more precise. The walking should be like a metronome, one length must be measured in exactly nine seconds. The fade-out at the end of Part I begins with the third step from the left, so that it is dark after the ninth step, i.e. in seven seconds. The mother speaks her text at the end of Part I on certain definite steps of May's. The first "May" comes on the fourth step while May is walking from right to left, the second "May" on the eighth step. May says her "Yes. Mother" on the fourth step when she is walking from left to right and on

the sixth step of the same stretch, the mother begins with "Will you never have done?" The sentence ends immediately before the turn. During the next length (from right to left) the mother begins on the second step with "Will you never have done revolving it all?" and ends before the turn on the left.[13]

Again, the only task of the first part of *Footfalls* is to offer a presentation of footsteps and that which remains beyond them, testifying to their failure to fill the hole of non-life, a presentation of the pure form of dialogue reduced to the minimum, in which the characters stop being indifferent only at the moment when they come across the real of "it all," of the unutterable cause of the steps. But it is precisely the fact that nothing spectacular is uttered in this dialogue that makes us all the more alert to the elements that almost imperceptibly dynamize this dialogue.

We have presupposed that these dynamics can be sought only on the terrain of the pause—and, in order to evade arbitrariness, we have to first notice the pauses as such, that is, notice their presence *and* their absence.

The pauses are of two kinds: the ones within and the ones between individual lines—and it is the latter that are crucial. If we read the initial lines, we can see that the exchange between May and her mother's voice proceeds more or less as we would expect. After the repeated call, the mother slowly responds. Once the connection between the two worlds is established, a somewhat warped, distorted, but nevertheless stable homeliness emerges in which the exchange of lines is interrupted only by the moments of May's hesitance.

M: Would you like me to inject you again?

V: Yes, but it is too soon.

[*Pause.*]

M: Would you like me to change your position again?

V: Yes, but it is too soon.

[*Pause.*]

M: Straighten your pillows? [*Pause.*] Change your drawsheet? [*Pause.*] Pass you the bedpan? [*Pause.*] The warming-pan? [*Pause.*] Dress your sores? [*Pause.*] Sponge you down? [*Pause.*] Moisten your poor lips? [*Pause.*] Pray with you? [*Pause.*] For you? [*Pause.*] Again.

[*Pause.*]

V: Yes, but it is too soon.

[*Pause.*][14]

The first pause between the lines, dictated by the mother's voice, appears only before the last "Yes, but it is too soon." And this is precisely the point that is followed by a minimal turn, which we notice not because of the presence of the pause but precisely because of its absence:

M: What age am I now?

V: And I? [*Pause. No louder.*] And I?[15]

The voice that has so far expressed a sort of a structural altruism—assuming the position of a person that both takes care of and is taken care of—at this point surprises us with a hint of strange aliveness, a hint of unexpected egoism, some sort of quasi-subjectivity, that puts the continuation of Part I in a completely different light and sets up the terrain for the rest of the play, in which the figure of the mother obtains a barely perceptible but therefore all the more intense eeriness.

Of course, once we have noticed the shift, there can arise the impression that the dynamical moment, the surprising absence of a pause that brings an unexpected change of rhythm, is only an auxiliary element that at best merely emphasizes the clear message in the content. To dispel this impression, it suffices to apply this practical test: could the line be understood in this way if we placed a pause before it?

M:  What age am I now?
[*Pause.*]
V:  And I? [*Pause. No louder.*] And I?[16]

The difference is minimal, but still, if this exchange were written so, we would lose the formal moment that not only stresses the point but co-creates it. The line could, in a way, still be interpreted as the moment when the mother whom we expected to be focused purely on her daughter's troubles is caught in a moment of insensitivity. But if this could still be seen as egoism, we would consider it to be the egoism of a demented old woman rambling in her world—just as May rambles in hers. Egoism in question here, however, is egoism of the mother's *voice*, egoism of an *object*, an uncanny return of all too human psychology in the completely de-humanized universe.

Again, what we would lose with the introduction of the pause would be the effect of an intrusion, an invasion—and it is this effect that first turns the line into an intrusion of another time *before the beginning* that is indeterminately inscribed into "it all" to which May's steps are responding. It is only the egoism of this type—whose construction is, for lack of other expressive means, wholly dependent on the radicalness of the *non-pause*, the mechanical immediateness impossible in interpersonal communication—that captures the real of the relation between both characters and turns Part I of *Footfalls* into a full-blooded prelude to what follows in the rest of the play: a presentation of psychical "abode" in the precise Beckettian sense, a presentation of a singular space of fully materialized psyche that is not simply closed, isolated from the outside world, but is *exclusively interior*, an "inside" without an "outside," a space, which, as sheer interior, represents the interior as well as the exterior.

Above, we have pointed out the particular status of pauses between the lines—of objective, structural pauses, *and* non-pauses, delineating relations between different layers of sound and speech. In a rather similar manner, the entire effort of the play *That Time*, in which three different voices (A, B, and C) belonging to the same person successively pass from one to another, aims precisely at utterly minimizing all of the explicitly undesignated pauses within each individual intervention (here Beckett insisted on pure *legato*), as well as within transitions between the voices. These—as stated in the introductory note—should be performed without interruption, "without solution of continuity," however, the switch from one voice to another should be "clearly faintly perceptible." And it is precisely this type of objective pause that plays a central role in the 1981 dramaticule *Ohio Impromptu*, a short piece in which Beckett staged, so to speak, nothing but the pure mechanism of staging.[17]

The scene of *Ohio Impromptu* is fairly simple. On stage, there is a table at which—similarly to a reading rehearsal—two men are seated: *Listener* and *Reader*. The two, as Beckett had noted, are "as alike in appearance as possible."[18] However, contrary to what could have been expected, they do not mirror each other. "The image is a counterfeit rather than a counterpart; what we see is a near-double instead of a doppelgänger."[19]

After ten seconds, Reader turns the page—and immediately we are witness to the central dynamics and the central formal subject:

R:   *Reading*. Little is left to tell. In a last–
[*L knocks with left hand on table.*]
Little is left to tell.
[*Pause. Knock.*]
In a last attempt to obtain relief[20]

The coordinates are set, and all that follows is characterized by similar exchanges: Reader's knocking, which dictates the dynamics of reading, or, more precisely, the dynamics of the pause, whereby the first knock appears to be an interruption, and the second one the permission to continue. But even though all subsequent repetitions that follow are, in principle, very much alike, a slight difference between them is nevertheless noticeable. In the mentioned fragment—its structure is later repeated a couple of times—the first knock appears at the moment when Reader wishes to continue reading without making a pause; in this sense, the knock is nothing but a correction, a demand to insert a pause which would enable a particularly significant line to be perceived as such. However, later in the text, there is another variation of the same intervention, which introduces a slightly modified configuration.

> Then turn and his slow steps retrace.
> [*Pause.*]
> In his dreams–
> [*Knock.*]
> Then turn and his slow steps retrace.
> [*Pause. Knock.*]
>
> In his dreams he had been warned against this change.[21]

Again, in the first variation, Listener's interruption occurred during a sentence, which directly followed a previous one without being preceded by a pause. In the second variation, however, Listener interrupts despite the fact that a pause had already been inserted. Whereas in the first variation, the knock occurred as a reaction to the absence of a pause, demanding its insertion, in the second variation what Listener aims at is no longer so unambiguous.

This difference can undoubtedly be interpreted in several different ways, and we might even content ourselves with the fact that here Reader only attempts to correct the insufficient length of the pause, his latter gesture being just a variation of the first one; nevertheless, the fact that the difference is objectively operational—perhaps not when reading, but definitely when staging it—still remains. And it is precisely this minimal modification that not only disrupts the bare monotony and pattern of which one could soon grow weary but also produces a minimum of temporal direction, minimal orientation toward the end.

> The sad tale a last time told.
> [*Pause.*]
> Nothing is left to tell.
> [*Pause. R makes to close book.*
> *Knock. Book half closed.*]
> Nothing is left to tell.
> [*Pause. R closes book.*
> *Knock.*
> *Silence. Five seconds.*
> *Simultaneously they lower their right hands to table, raise their heads and look at each other. Unblinking. Expressionless.*
> *Ten seconds.*
> *Fade out.*][22]

In the universe of time that has turned into space, in the universe that has been deprived of all the ordinary means and reasons to come to an end, the dynamics can only be generated within what is usually considered as the materialization of stasis and monotony. When *little is left to tell* expires into *nothing is left to tell*, the only thing left is to affirm the pause itself in becoming no louder.

# Notes

1   Samuel Beckett, "Endgame," in *The Complete Dramatic Works* (London: Faber and Faber, 1990), 98.

2  Samuel Beckett, "Footfalls," in *The Complete Dramatic Works* (London: Faber and Faber, 1990), 400.

3  Samuel Beckett, "Not I," in *The Complete Dramatic Works* (London: Faber and Faber, 1990), 378.

4  Samuel Beckett, *Malone Dies*, ed. Peter Boxall (London: Faber and Faber, 2009), 32–3.

5  Samuel Beckett, "Ohio Impromptu," in *The Complete Dramatic Works* (London: Faber and Faber, 1990), 445.

6  Beckett, "Footfalls," 400.

7  Beckett, "Endgame," 95, 98.

8  Beckett, "Footfalls," 399–400.

9  Ibid., 399.

10  Ibid.

11  Walter Asmus, "Rehearsal Notes for the German Premiere of Beckett's *That Time* and *Footfalls*," in *On Beckett: Essays and Criticism*, ed. Stanley E. Gontarski (London/New York: Anthem Press, 2012), 254.

12  Ibid.

13  Ibid., 256.

14  Beckett, "Footfalls," 399–400.

15  Ibid., 400.

16  Ibid.

17  For a beautiful reading of the interstice between form and content, cf. Sara Jane Bailes, "*Ohio Impromptu*: Reading Blanchot, Hearing Beckett," in *Beckett and Musicality*, ed. Sara Jane Bailes and Nicholas Till (Farnham: Ashgate, 2014), 199–213.

18  Beckett, "Ohio Impromptu," 445.

19  Enoch Brater, *Beyond Minimalism: Beckett's Later Style in the Theater* (Oxford: Oxford University Press, 1987), 31.

20  Beckett, "Ohio Impromptu," 445.

21  Beckett, "Ohio Impromptu," 446.

22  Beckett, "Ohio Impromptu," 448.

# Bibliography

Asmus, Walter. "Rehearsal Notes for the German Premiere of Beckett's *That Time* and *Footfalls*." In *On Beckett: Essays and Criticism*, edited by Stanley E. Gontarski, 253–64. London/New York: Anthem Press, 2014.

Bailes, Sara Jane. "*Ohio Impromptu*: Reading Blanchot, Hearing Beckett." In *Beckett and Musicality*, edited by Sara Jane Bailes and Nicholas Till, 199–213. Farnham: Ashgate, 2014.

Beckett, Samuel. "Endgame." In *The Complete Dramatic Works*, 89–134. London: Faber and Faber, 2006.

Beckett, Samuel. "Footfalls." In *The Complete Dramatic Works*, 397–403. London: Faber and Faber, 2006.

Beckett, Samuel. "Not I." In *The Complete Dramatic Works*, 373–83. London: Faber and Faber, 2006.

Beckett, Samuel. "Ohio Impromptu." In *The Complete Dramatic Works*, 443–8. London: Faber and Faber, 2006.

Beckett, Samuel. *Malone Dies*, edited by Peter Boxall. London: Faber and Faber, 2010.

Brater, Enoch. *Beyond Minimalism: Beckett's Later Style in the Theater*. Oxford: Oxford University Press, 1987.

# NOTES ON CONTRIBUTORS

**Alain Badiou** is a mathematician, a playwright, a novelist, and a political activist, but is certainly best known as one of the world's leading philosophers. He formerly held the Chair of Philosophy at the Institute of Philosophy at the École Normale Superieure in Paris and holds the René Descartes Chair of Philosophy at the European Graduate School in Saas Fee.

**Rebecca Comay** is Professor of Philosophy and Comparative Literature and Director of the Program in Literary Studies at the University of Toronto. She is the author of numerous articles and of *Mourning Sickness: Hegel and the French Revolution* (Stanford, CA: Stanford University Press, 2011) and together with Frank Ruda of *The Dash—The Other Side of Absolute Knowing* (Cambridge, MA: MIT Press, 2018).

**Mladen Dolar** is Professor of Philosophy at the University of Ljubljana and, together with Slavoj Žižek, he is one of the founders of what is known to be the "Ljubljana School of Psychoanalysis." His main fields of expertise are German Idealism—especially Hegel—and French Structuralism. Together with Slavoj Žižek he is the author of *Opera's Second Death* (London: Routledge, 2001) and of a seminal book on the voice, entitled *A Voice and Nothing More* (Cambridge, MA: MIT Press, 2006).

**Eva Heubach** is a Postdoctoral Fellow at the Centre for Comparative Literature at the University of Toronto, Canada.

**Tadej Troha** is a research fellow at the Research Centre of the Slovenian Academy of Sciences and Arts in Ljubljana. He is the author of several articles on psychoanalysis, politics, and literature and of *Neither Miracle Nor Miracle* (Ljubljana: Analecta 2011).

**Philipp Weber** is a research assistant at the Institute for German Literature at Ruhr-Universität Bochum. He is the author of *Kosmos und Subjektivität in der Frühromantik* (Paderborn: Fink, 2017).

# INDEX

Adorno, Theodor W. 47, 57 n.38, 62, 83, 95 n.22, 134 n.50, 134 n.53, 136 n.75
  *The Actuality of Philosophy* 119–20, 136 n.65
  *Aesthetic Theory* 78–9, 81, 97 n.38, 119, 120, 121–2, 135 n.64, 136 n.67, 136 n.71, 136 n.72, 136 n.74
  *Dialectic of Enlightenment*, with Max Horkheimer 168 n.49
  *Eine Fernsehdiskussion über Samuel Beckett* 121, 136 n.69
  *Extorted Reconciliation* 116, 122, 134 n.54, 134 n.55, 136 n.73
  *Graeculus (II)* 117, 135 n.57, 136 n.71
  and Hegel, G.W.F. 119–20
  *History and Freedom* 98 n.52
  and Lukács, Georg 115–17, 119–23, 127–8, 134 n.51, 136 n.73, 137 n.77, 57 n.38
  *Minima Moralia* 120, 136 n.66
  *Negative Dialectics* 81, 98 n.44, 120, 136 n.68
  *Notes on Kafka* 98 n.45
  *Notes on The Unnamable* 137 n.77
  *Titles* 2, 8 n.1
  *Trying to Understand Endgame* 79, 97 n.40, 116, 119, 121, 136 n.70, 156, 168 n.50
  *Wagner's Relevance for Today* 96 n.33
Agamben, Giorgio 163 n.6, 166 n.31
Alexander, Archibald 94 n.12
Anouilh, Jean 57 n.48

Badiou, Alain 31, 36, 40, 56 n.27, 57 n.38, 57 n.40, 58 n.54, 123, 137 n.76, 153, 166 n.35, 167 n.45, 168 n.59
Balibar, Étienne 164 n.8

Balzac, Honoré de 129 n.6
Barthes, Roland 163 n.1
Bataille, Georges 96 n.27
Beckett, Samuel
  *Breath* 99 n.58
  *Comment C'est* 39, 52, 131 n.17
  *Dante … Bruno. Vico.. Joyce* 30, 138 n.89
  *Dream of Fair to Middling Women* 124, 128 n.1
  *Embers* 138 n.84
  *Endgame* 14, 54, 56 n.23, 68, 70, 73, 78, 87, 95 n.24, 96 n.29, 96 n.31, 99 n.60, 133 n.48, 176, 191 n.1
  *Enough* 22, 23
  *Film* 42
  *Footfalls* 77, 80, 85–6, 97 n.41, 99 n.57, 173, 177–88, 192 n.2, 192 n.8, 192 n.14
  *German Letter* 3–5, 8 n.3, 31, 32, 37, 55 n.11, 55 n.13
  *Gnome* 95 n.17
  *Happy Days* 14, 35, 99 n.59
  *How It Is* 11, 12, 13, 20, 52, 68, 77, 78, 131 n.17
  *Ill Seen Ill Said* 12–24
  *Krapp's Last Tape* 14, 27–9, 54 n.1, 54 n.2, 54 n.5
  *La Fin* 55 n.16
  *The Lost Ones* 11, 13, 39, 52
  *Le Dépeupleur* 39, 52
  *Lessness* 88, 99 n.63
  *L'Innommable* 108–14, 123, 131 n.17, 133 n.46
  *Malone Dies* 35, 36, 47, 48, 56 n.28, 68, 108, 175, 192 n.4
  *Malone meurt* 108, 109

*Mercier and Camier* 32–41, 43, 46–8, 55 n.18, 55 n.19, 56 n.22, 56 n.24, 56 n.26, 56 n.29, 56 n.30, 56 n.33, 57 n.39, 46, 58 n.50, 108
*Mercier et Camier* 32, 35, 56 n.25, 58 n.52, 108, 125, 129 n.7, 133 n.46
*Molloy* 11, 13, 29, 48, 54 n.3, 77, 108, 109, 130 n.12, 130 n.13, 138 n.82
*More Pricks than Kicks* 129 n.1
*Murphy* 13, 30, 38, 42, 53, 58 n.66, 67, 97 n.34, 106, 108, 124, 126, 128 n.1, 129 n.2, 131 n.14, 132 n.17
Not-I 174, 192 n.3
*Ohio Impromptu* 176, 189, 192 n.5, 192 n.18, 192 n.20
*A Piece of Monologue* 77, 176
*Ping* 53, 58 n.62
*Philosophy Notes* 64–5, 69, 93 n.9, 94 n.13
*Proust* 110
*Quad* 99 n.66, 176
revelation 27–31, 34
*Rockaby* 176
*Sans* 88
*Stirrings Still* 13, 166
*Suite* 55 n.16
*Têtes Mortes* 53, 58 n.62
*Texts for Nothing* 165 n.28
*That Time* 176, 188
*The Unnamable* 8, 9 n.11, 11, 35, 38, 47, 48–50, 56 n.35, 58 n.56, 68, 108–14, 123, 127, 131 n.15, 131 n.17, 133 n.43, 138 n.87, 138 n.88
*Waiting for Godot* 14, 40, 47, 77, 98 n.54, 175, 176
*Watt* 11, 13, 16, 42, 54 n.8, 55 n.16, 57 n.43, 62, 77, 92 n.4, 106, 108, 109, 129 n.3, 143–5, 151–62, 164 n.9, 166 n.29, 166 n.30, 166 n.34, 166 n.37, 167 n.41, 167 n.44, 168 n.48, 168 n.53, 168 n.54, 168 n.58, 169 n.65, 169 n.70

*What Where* 78
*Whoroscope* 169 n.59
*Worstward Ho* 18, 31, 55 n.12
Benjamin, Walter 67–8, 79, 95 n.20, 95 n.21, 95 n.22
Bergson, Henri 166 n.32
Blanchot, Maurice 169 n.63
Blankenburg, Friedrich von 145
Blanqui, Auguste 67, 95 n.20
Blumenberg, Hans 163 n.1
Breton, André 96 n.27
Burnet, John 94 n.12

Campe, Rüdiger 145, 154, 163 n.1, 163 n.2, 163 n.4, 167 n.42, 167 n.43
Cassirer, Ernst 93 n.9
Comay, Rebecca 96 n.33, 98 n.46, 99 n.65, 138 n.90
Connor, Steven 55 n.17

Dante 16, 36–7, 56 n.29, 56 n.31
Descartes, René 93 n.9, 164 n.8
Deleuze, Gilles 32, 57 n.38, 82, 98 n.47, 98 n.49, 98 n.50, 166 n.32
Dolar, Mladen 62, 92 n.2, 106, 129 n.4, 138 n.87, 165 n.16

Engels, Friedrich 100 n.71
Etchell, Tim 45

Flaubert, Gustave 44, 46, 66–7
Fratellini Brothers 57 n.48
Freud, Sigmund 44, 148–9, 165 n.17, 165 n.20

Geulen, Eva 98 n.51, 128, 139 n.91, 163 n.6
Goethe, Johann Wolfgang von 166 n.33
Graevenitz, Gerhart von 164 n.7
Guattari, Felix 32

Hegel, G.W.F. 6, 61–2, 69, 80, 87, 99 n.64, 115, 118
   *Aesthetics* 90–2, 100 n.67, 100 n.68, 128
   *Phenomenology of Spirit* 9 n.10, 68–9, 71–3, 75, 91, 95 n.25, 96 n.27, 96 n.32, 100 n.70, 117, 119–20, 135 n.58

*Philosophy of Right* 53–4, 58 n.64,
    88–90, 99 n.64, 99 n.66
*Science of Logic* 91, 100 n.69
Heidegger, Martin 54 n.7
Henrich, Dieter 54 n.8
Hölderlin, Friedrich 30, 54 n.8, 62

Jameson, Fredric 9 n.10, 123, 135 n.59,
    136 n.73, 136 n.75, 137 n.77
Jean Paul 57 n.49
Johns, Jasper 92
Joyce, James 30–1, 37, 61, 118, 124–5, 127

Kafka, Franz 118, 167 n.43
Kant, Immanuel 69, 93 n.9, 94 n.15, 146,
    147, 164 n.9, 164 n.10, 164 n.11
Kleist, Heinrich von 42
Kojève, Alexandre 69, 96 n.27

Lacan, Jacques 8 n.2, 96 n.27, 96 n.30, 134
    n.49, 149, 160, 165 n.20, 165 n.21,
    165 n.22, 169 n.62
Lecercle, Jean-Jacques 57 n.38
Leiris, Michel 96 n.27
Lévi-Strauss, Claude 155, 167 n.47
Lukács, Georg
    and Adorno, Theodor W. 115–17,
        119–23, 127–8, 134 n.51, 136
        n.73, 137 n.77, 57 n.38
    *Brief über die Budapester Schule* 134
        n.51
    *The Destruction of Reason* 116
    and Hegel, G.W.F. 117, 118
    *History and Class Consciousness* 117,
        135 n.59
    *The Meaning of Contemporary Realism*
        118, 135 n.60, 167 n.46
    *Theory of the Novel* 34–5, 56 n.21, 117,
        135 n.56, 137 n.77, 147, 155, 164
        n.12, 164 n.13, 164 n.14, 164
        n.15, 166 n.32, 167 n.46
Loraux, Nicole 134 n.49

Malevich, Kasimir 92
Mann, Thomas 167 n.43
Marx, Karl 78, 92, 100 n.71

Mauthner, Fritz 93 n.9
Mallarmé 16, 55 n.15
Martial, Marcus Valerius 134 n.48
McNaughton, James 78
Merleau-Ponty, Maurice 96 n.27
Molièr 42
Moretti, Franco 163 n.1

Nietzsche, Friedrich 80, 82, 98 n.42, 98
    n.48
Novalis 145, 163 n.3

Ovid 57 n.41, 96 n.28, 134 n.48

Pascal 14, 42, 45, 57 n.48
Plautus 42

Queneau, Raymond 96 n.27

Reinhardt, Ad 92
Richardson, Brian 48, 58 n.55
Richter, Gerhard 92
Ruda, Frank 96 n.33, 138 n.90
Ryman, Robert 92

Santner, Eric 167 n.41
Sartre, Jean-Paul 44, 66
Saussure, Ferdinand de 9 n.9
Schestag, Thomas 129 n.6
Schlegel, Friedrich 65, 163 n.5
Scholem, Gershom 67, 95 n.22
Schopenhauer, Arthur 65, 93 n.9
Shakespeare 42
Szondi, Peter 164 n.7

Van Velde, Bram 97 n.36

Walser, Robert 167 n.43
Wellbery, David 163 n.1
Windelband, Wilhelm 64, 67, 69, 94 n.12

Žižek, Slavoj 30, 54 n.7, 62, 92 n.2, 135
    n.59, 149–50, 164 n.9, 165 n.16, 165
    n.23, 165 n.24, 165 n.25, 165 n.26,
    168 n.53

Zupančič, Alenka 165 n.16

www.ingramcontent.com/pod-product-compliance
Lightning Source LLC
Chambersburg PA
CBHW070637300426
44111CB00013B/2149